Chiara Lubich

Early Letters
At the Origins of a
New Spirituality

Translated and with a Foreword
by
Bill Hartnett

New City Press
Hyde Park, New York

Published in the United States by New City Press
202 Comforter Blvd., Hyde Park, NY 12538
www.newcitypress.com
©2012 New City Press (English Translation)

Translated by Bill Hartnett from the original Italian
Lettere dei primi tempi
©2010 Città Nuova Editrice, Rome, Italy

Cover design by Durva Correia

Biblical citations are taken from the *New Revised Standard Version*
©1989 Division of Christian Education of the National Council of Churches of Christ
in the United States of America.

Library of Congress Cataloging-in-Publication Data
Lubich, Chiara, 1920-2008.
    [Lettere dei primi tempi, 1943-1949. English]
    Early letters : at the origins of a new spirituality / Chiara Lubich ; translated and with a foreword by Bill Hartnett.
        p. cm.
    Includes bibliographical references.
    ISBN 978-1-56548-432-0 (pbk. : alk. paper) 1. Catholics--Italy--Correspondence. 2. Focolare Movement. I. Title.
    BX4705.L792A4 2012
    267'.182092--dc23
                    2012002280

Printed in the United States of America

Contents

Foreword

On occasions when Chiara would reluctantly speak about her own role in the founding of the Focolare Movement, she would usually share a little anecdote that went something like this: When the painter takes up his brush, the brush has no idea of what it will paint. It is merely an instrument in the hands of the artist. It's the artist who creates the masterpiece. When the sculptor takes up the chisel, the chisel has no notion of what it will carve. A pen in the hand of a writer has no idea of what it will write. When asked about her role in this work of God, Chiara would always direct the attention away from herself and place it in God. Nevertheless, it must be recognized that Chiara was always completely open to the promptings of the Holy Spirit and courageously obedient to the voice of God. She fully cooperated with the many special graces given to her by God for her task as the founder of a new work of God in the Church and in the world.

In the preface to the original Italian edition of this book, Chiara is called a great Catholic mystic of our time. Mystics are those individuals whom God allows to have a unique experience of communion with God, and insight into the things of God. In these letters we encounter this mystical side of Chiara who is also the bearer of a charism, a gift from the Holy Spirit in response to the special needs of the Church and of the world. Chiara's charism is unity, the unity that Jesus asked for us from his Father: "May they be one as we are one — I in them and you in me — so that they may be brought to complete unity" (Jn 17: 22-23).

In July of 1942, Father Casimiro Perarolo, the newly appointed director of the Capuchin Third Order, was invited by another friar to visit the young Third Order member named Sylvia (Chiara) Lubich at the Franciscan orphanage in Trent. She had been working there as an elementary school teacher for the past year. Father Casimiro not only spoke to Chiara, but also visited her in her classroom on the day of his departure. He asked her to offer an hour of her workday to God, for his apostolate. "Only an hour?" she asked. "And why not the whole day?" The priest was surprised by her generous answer and spontaneously responded. Inviting Chiara to kneel down, he blessed her saying: "Miss, remember: God loves you immensely."

This sentence spoken by the priest resounded through Chiara's entire being. She continued to repeat it: "God loves me immensely, God loves me immensely ..." She said of that moment, that it was as if she had been struck by lightning. She felt urged to tell it to her sisters, her mother, her father, and then to some friends: "God loves you immensely, God loves us immensely."

From that day forward, she saw God's love everywhere. Everything and everyone was a manifestation of his love. On that day, Chiara's life took a step forward. The light of this discovery enveloped her and she felt like she was at the center of a Father's love. This discovery is at the foundation of Chiara's spirituality which emerges from these early letters. They were written to the young women and others who were drawn by the way she presented the Christian life as a response to God's love, which was shown to her in Jesus, most especially in his abandonment and death on the Cross. In these letters, the God that Chiara invites us to believe in is Love. The conversion she asks of us is a conversion to Love.

Often using the unfamiliar language and style of the saints and mystics of other ages (like Saint Catherine of Siena and Saint Francis of Assisi), Chiara communicates her burning desire that "Love be loved," that "the whole world be set ablaze by the fire of Love." Her words are full of fervor, but also simplicity and practical common sense. Faith in God's love leads to faith in his mercy. This is another striking theme of Chiara's thinking which comes across in these early letters. Mercy is the main quality of God's love for us, she says. Therefore, we should turn to him in trust, offering our shortcomings and sins, knowing that they are the only things that are truly ours. She reminds her own sister that Jesus is a Savior and, as such, wants nothing more than to save, to forgive, to consume our failures in the fire of his mercy.

In December 1943, while fetching some milk at the White Madonna farm, Chiara felt that God said to her: "Give yourself to me." She was so struck by these words that she stood frozen in her tracks for a moment in the middle of the road. And then in her heart she answered: "Yes, right away." A few days later, with the permission of her confessor, she consecrated her life to God on December 7. For her, it meant marrying God. "Imagine," she would later write, "a young woman in love for the first time, only that she can't see her beloved with the eyes of this world. She can't see him or hear him or touch him. She can't enjoy his fragrance with the senses of her body, but with those of the soul, through which Love — with a capital L — has entered in and totally invaded her entire being. And she experiences joys that are impossible to experience in the life of this earth."[1]

She first shared the news of this secret joy with Doriana Zamboni, who would become one of the first focolarinas and whom Chiara was tutoring at the time. A month later, on January 24, 1944, while Chiara was assisting Doriana whose face had been infected when she was helping a poor woman, a priest arrived with Holy Communion. As he was leaving, he turned to Chiara and asked: "When do you think Jesus suffered the most?" Chiara responded that she had always heard that it was in the Garden of Olives when he sweated blood. But the priest disagreed. "I think it was when he cried out on the Cross: 'My God, my God, why have you forsaken me?'" It was another lightning bolt. Chiara turned to her ailing companion and said: Since this is when Jesus suffered most, then it's also when he loved us most. Then let us choose him as our portion in life. From that moment on Jesus forsaken would be the "spouse," the "bridegroom," the "Love" of Chiara's life. And she did everything she could to make others love him. At first she saw him in the empty and abandoned churches, then in the "sin-ridden" faces of people around her, in the suffering and needy, in her own limitations, in disunity, and especially in those who seem far from God.

Ever since the first air-raids over Trent in the fall of 1943, Chiara and her small group of companions would meet in the air-raid shelters, bringing with them a small copy of the Gospels. There, they would open the book at random and read those words that Chiara called luminous and illuminated by a divine and supernatural light that shone beneath them. But she also called them words of "life." For Chiara, reading or meditating on the Word of God was never the main point, but putting it into practice in daily life. And they did this together, by choosing the same phrase to live each day and then reporting back to each other how it went. It was this practice of the Word of Life that drew people into the new community that was

1. Armando Torno, *PortarTi il mondo fra le braccia, vita di Chiara Lubich* (Rome: Città Nuova Editrice, 2011), p. 21.

being created around Chiara and her companions. For Chiara, the Word of Life was another presence of Jesus along with his presence in the Eucharist. Just as a tiny portion of the sacred host is enough to nourish us with the entire Jesus, she would say, so too, each word of the Gospel is enough to nourish us with the entire Jesus when we allow his Word to become "flesh" in us.

One day their eyes fell upon the new commandment of Jesus in John 15:12. Realizing that they could die at any moment because of the bombs, they had asked themselves if there were something they could do before they died, that would be particularly pleasing to God. They opened the Gospels and read: "My command is this: love each other as I have loved you." For Chiara, love of neighbor was always central to her understanding of religion. "Measure your love for God by the love that you bring to your neighbor" she writes in Letter 38. But this was a different expression of love. Here Jesus was asking for mutual love among Christians. Chiara calls this "new" commandment, which Jesus calls his own, the "Pearl of the Gospel." And she approaches it in a practical way, by making a solemn pact with her closest companions in which they promise each other to be ready to give up their lives for each other. Although this promise never involved giving up their physical lives, it could be lived in a practical way by giving up anything less — time, energy, personal ideas, preferences, etc.

Through the practice of the new commandment, Chiara uncovers another presence of Jesus: "Where two or more gather in my name, there am I with them" (Mt 18:20). This opened a new horizon for Chiara. Now Jesus had truly become the Light of their life. For Chiara, this presence was also a real mystical presence of Jesus. People began calling the "little house" where she and some of her first companions were living at 2 Capuchin Plaza, the "hearth." This particular presence of Jesus among those united in his name, in his love, Chiara would later explain, is something that can be perceived. The "Fire" of this mystical hearth was Jesus himself, and many people's hearts were drawn and transformed by his Warmth, and evangelized by his Light.

When Jesus is among us, he makes us one in him. We experience unity, unity that is a share in the divine life of the Holy Trinity. Jesus commanded us to love each other, Chiara once said, but he prayed that we would be one — one as he and the Father are one. Unity is the gift of Jesus among us. It's not something we gain through our own efforts. And it's a gift that's given to "two or more." It pre-supposes that there is a community of Christians who live the "self-emptying" and "dying-to-self" love which is lived in the Trinity. But it is Jesus, who, with his presence among us, obtains the gift of unity for us. For Chiara, unity is the culmination and goal of the spiritual life; it's the life of the Trinity on earth. In Letter 46 she writes: "Unity in the beginning, in the middle, and in the end." "… just as in the most Holy Trinity." And in Letter 44: "Unity! But who would dare speak of it? It's ineffable as God! You feel it, you enjoy it … but it's ineffable! Everyone enjoys its presence. It's peace, gladness, love, ardor, an atmosphere of heroism, of complete generosity. It's Jesus among us!" But unity is also the beginning of the spiritual life for Chiara: Unity comes before everything, she writes in Letter 56, even if that "everything" involves the most sacred things like praying, celebrating Mass, etc.

Chiara wants everyone to be drawn into this unity. "Ask me, and I will make the nations your inheritance, the ends of the earth your possession (Ps 2:8)." After hearing these words read on the feast of Christ the King, October 1945, she immediately gathered with the small group of her companions. Kneeling around an altar, they asked Jesus to use them to bring the unity he desired for all, to the farthest corners of the world. And so it happened. In just a couple of months, there was already a community of 500 people sharing Chiara's spirituality of unity in Trent and it quickly spread to other lands, entering into other Churches, religions and cultures.

Mary is very present in Chiara's spiritual life right from the beginning. In Letter 28 Chiara writes that Our Lady is happy seeing us focused on this desire of her Son. In Letter 36 it is Mary who wants us united, with Jesus in our midst. In the same letter it is Mary who has "brought us together." In Letter 31, a group of focolarinas preparing to consecrate their lives to God, have been drawn by "the sweet voice of the Mother, the Immaculate Virgin." In Letter 49, she refers to core group of the focolarinas as the "Mary Unity," an identity that would later be assigned to the entire Movement. Chiara once remarked that even though the charism of unity was given by the Holy Spirit, in this case, Mary had a big hand in it. The Movement bears her name: Work of Mary, because Chiara saw the Movement as a presence of Mary on earth, almost her "continuation," as is written in Article 2 of the revised General Statutes of the Work of Mary which were approved by the Holy See in 1990.[2] In Letters 35, 37, 46, and 59, Mary is the "Mother of Unity." She is the one in whom the divine nature was first united to our human nature. She is the one who takes pleasure in seeing her Son being reborn among us, and who wants to "consume us in one" when we are gathered in his name.

The language style of these letters is informal, spontaneous and conversational. At times the letters are written in pencil or on the back of a used envelope. Chiara wrote these letters in the midst of the War and during the reconstruction that followed. Some were penned as the bombs were falling around her. Her language is that of the Italian 1940's. Therefore, she does not use gender-sensitive language and she often refers to people as "souls." At times, she uses a Franciscan vocabulary with words such as "Seraphic," which can mean "heavenly glory" or "Franciscan." In this book her use of capitalization and punctuation has been respected. In some cases, her underlining of words has been preserved, otherwise it has been italicized.

Bill Hartnett

---

2. *Work of Mary: General Statutes* (New York: Focolare Movement, 2008), pp. 16-17.

"Whoever does not love does
not know God, for God is love"

(1 John 4:8).

L_{etter} 1

God Exists! Live For Him!

These words are from a letter written in early 1944 to some young people involved in the Franciscan Third Order.

Chiara, who was from Trent, inspired the souls of these young women who read her letters, which she signed using her simple Third Order name, Suor Chiara (Sister Clare).

"God," she writes, "Here is where the adventure begins."

"The word that God wanted me to express was himself: God."

These letters are the luminous documentation.

Ave Maria!

My Dearest Sisters,

I would like to be next to each one of you, speaking with my heart in my hand, with the delicateness of God, telling you in words that cut to the depths of the soul what is taking place in my heart. Sister, beautiful soul, also for you the Almighty has marked out a plan of love.

You too can live for something great in life. Believe it: God is in you!

Your soul in grace is a focal center for the Holy Spirit, the God who sanctifies.

Look inside you, search for God, your God, who lives in you.

Oh, if you only knew whom you have within you!

If only you would leave behind everything else for Him!

Oh, if only you would turn over to Him your life, which is brief as a sunset and escapes you with the passing of every new day!

Oh, if only God reigned in you and every power of your soul and body were a servant in the divine service to this King!

Oh, if only you loved Him with all your heart, all your mind, all your strength!

Then … you would fall in love with God and you would go through the world announcing the good news:

2

God exists! Live for Him!

God will be your judge! Live for Him!

God will be everything for you in a few years, after this brief life is over!

Throw yourself into him!

Love Him.

Listen to what He wants from you in every moment of your life!

Do it with all the enthusiasm of your hearts, consuming all your strength in this divine service.

Fall in love with God!

There are so many beautiful things on earth.

God is more beautiful!

Don't let your youth run away from you and amid the tears of a life that's failed you will have to say:

Late have I loved you!

Late have I loved you, oh beauty ever ancient, ever new!

No!

Still quivering with life, our blood is boiling within us!

Our heart still beats and can still love!

It can still prove its love by overcoming every hardship!

No!

I love you now my God, my all!

My All!

Command me now and I will do it! Your will is mine!

I want what You want!

Falling in love with God on earth means falling in love with his will!

Until our souls having lived in this divine service, will finally see Him and possess Him forever!

Sister Chiara

Letter 2

There's Only One Love

Letter dated January 30, 1944
to her sister Liliana

Chiara's younger sister was engaged to Paolo Berlanda who later became her husband. A few days before writing this letter on January 24, 1944, Chiara had met and chosen the one whom she called Jesus Forsaken. Strengthened with this discovery, she attempts to explain to her sister how she can also live as a fiancé fully devoted to God, for there is only one Love that will make her into another Christ by her self-denial. It is the first time that the word "Ideal" appears in one of these early letters. Chiara used this word to describe the light which she felt invested her from above and which she shared with those around her.

January 30, 1944

Lilianetta, My Little Sister,

Yesterday I told you I loved you and today I want to show it. I'll try to feed your soul with the Ideal, to make you rise with me all the way to Heaven: You for your way, I for mine.

Liliana, hear the cry of my heart: "Don't divide your heart here on earth, don't divide your Love!" There's only one Love, Liliana — one love, the love for God. But don't misunderstand me. Listen. There's one ideal in life that surpasses all others. It's contained in three things: Loving, making others love, and making reparation! This is my love and it should be yours if you wish to come along with me! Whom should you love? *God.* He lives in the hearts of all people. But since it is his will, you will have to see Him especially in one heart, the heart of Paolo! Liliana, you should love Paolo more than you love him now.

4

You know why? In Paolo you see God's Divine Will! You have to worship God who is dwelling in the heart of Paolo.

Understand:

Your love for God will be shown by loving Paolo *as much as you can*. For him, deny your selfishness, your desire to remain shut up in yourself, your personal comfort, all your faults. Increase your patience with him, your maternal grace. Know how to stay quiet when someone is wrong!

Above all, take instruction from only one book — and if only you would understand me as I wish you would — take instruction from the Crucified Jesus who was left abandoned by all and cried out: *"My God, my God, why have you forsaken me?"* Oh if only that divine face, twisted in pain, those eyes all bloodshot but gazing at you with such kindness, forgetting our sins that reduced Him to such conditions, were always in front of your eyes: How much more *you would love Paolo*!

You love him too little, much too little. *He is God for you; he's the will of God.* If you love Paolo much as to die for him, you love God, because (I repeat it, so that you can fix it in your mind) Paolo is *the expression of God* for you on earth!

There will be joys, sorrows, anxieties, but if you strive to see Jesus in him as I am presenting Him to you — and I always present Him in the culmination of suffering which is the apex of love — oh, then, my Liliana, your love for him will have no end not even in Heaven, because, in him, you don't love him, the man of flesh and bones, but you love God! Only in this way will your love become great. It must grow!

If you love Paolo little, then you love God little!

Remember Saint Rita? How did she love her Paolo? She didn't bear with all the insults so that he would convert, but only because she saw in this a manifestation of the Divine Will! She saw God in it!

Oh Liliana! Hold on to these words, read them over and over again, until you feel that you understand them completely. If you understood them, my heart would be content as it is watching out for you, fearing that you might suffer at the thought of your love being divided! No! No! There is only one Love! For you it is to love God in your Paolo. Become worthy of him as if you had to become worthy of God! Exactly like that! Oh it would be so easy for you to go through the world like an angel! Don't allow the world to spoil the purity of your heart; your heart is for God and His will and, therefore, for Paolo, in whom you must see God! Lower your eyes, for they should sparkle only for Him and the world mustn't disturb you with its pitfalls. The hazards are many even for you, even though you are married. Go into the world soaring over and above all the ugliness! If your first love was God, then humbly thank him, for you weren't worthy of such a gift! Feel your weakness in front of such a gift, your misery, your nothing-ness — and sing, sing loud the anthem of Love.

"Be praised, my Lord, through Paolo, in whom I love and admire your Divine Will!"[1]

My Liliana, learn to love! Pray for me often. This would be the great-est gift you could give me. But, above all, pray for Paolo. God com-mands you: Pray for Paolo and love God. Pray to God that you can understand this Ideal that gathers in everyone, and pray that Paolo understands it. Now, perhaps, you don't have it so clearly, no, no! But I'll explain more.

Your Silvietta,
who loves you with undying affection.

Perfect Happiness

Letter of March 8, 1944 to Fosca Pellegrini

Fosca Pellegrini was a young woman from Albola on the Coast of Garda, who attended a meeting of Franciscan Ter-tiaries held by Chiara on Saturday afternoons in the Cardinal Massaia Hall, just above St. Mark's Church in Trent. Chiara barely knew Miss Pellegrini, yet with prudence and a bit of firm-

---

1. Imitation of the *Praise of the Creatures*, a song of praise attributed to St. Francis of Assisi.

ness — and motivated only by love — she becomes an advocate for God who wants to give the gift of perfect happiness to Fosca as well.

Trent, March 8, 1944

Dear Miss Pellegrini,

You probably can't even imagine who it is that writes you.

But perhaps you still remember: Trent, on the *San Marco Way*, a small dark hall, lots of cheerful and noisy young women who were assuring you that they had found "Perfect Joy."[2]

I'm one of them, Chiara — Silvia ... to the secular world — and I often remember you with fondness, and lost your address, and now that I've recovered it, I've hurried to write, because, from the day I met you, I felt kindly toward you! I was the one sitting near to the stove, the quiet one, a spectator of all those young and elderly people who were bound to each other by the unbreakable bond of brotherhood, of love, the Ideal, and Joy!

Oh, Miss Fosca! If only you were there for our meeting on Sunday! You would never have wanted to leave!

Up here, where the youth are all still sensitive to high Ideals, they're so ardent and generous!

The Ideal that we follow can make you dizzy and if we throw ourselves headlong into the Infinite Loving Arms of God whom we love in the most perfect joy, it's even staggering!

We feel a subtle nostalgia in our hearts for the Infinite, nostalgia for an ideal that would allow our hearts to say that they were full. Our mind is avid for Truth, for that Truth that doesn't pass away because it's Life!

Miss Fosca, if you were with us, close to Chiara who already loves you as a sister, you would have Perfect Happiness.

Each of us follows her path! The one that God has tracked out for us with marvelous Goodness and Wisdom! Each of us encounters her trials, but they're trials which, painful as they are, are embedded in a single act: Love!

---

2. This is a reference to Saint Francis of Assisi who refers to Jesus Crucified as perfect joy. See: Regis J. Armstrong, OFM Cap., Wayne J. A. Hellmann, OFM Conv., William J. Short, OFM (eds.), *The Prophet* (Francis of Assisi, Early Documents vol.3), New York: New City Press 2001), pp. 579–581.

Those among us who are most tried by the hand of God are those whose heart hears more the Voice of God and in whom this Ideal (which is peace and joy) is realized!

These are wonders worked in the lives of those who follow the footsteps of the Seraphic Jester of Christ, the Knight of Christ, the Minstrel of Creation![3]

Following Him every obstacle is ironed out; every suffering sweetens the bitterness, because He leads us along the straight path, along the luminous Road of the Gospel! There is joy and comfort to be had in the midst of so much human misery and vain concern for *"Christ's little madwomen!"* Because we already love Jesus. For Him and with Him we crush beneath our feet the bitter seeds that the world would sow in our hearts!

Perhaps my little letter surprises you!

It is love that makes me speak.

I think: Why can't a joy so great as the one in my heart also enter the heart of Miss Pellegrini? It wasn't for nothing that the Lord allowed me to make your acquaintance. Because I believe that a soul never touches our own in vain.

That's why I wrote to you.

Perhaps you won't mind. No, no! I saw in your eyes, in your smile, a deep desire for Goodness, Love, and Happiness!

Write to me, Miss Pellegrini, and call me by my Franciscan name, Chiara. We can dispense with the "Miss!"

I don't see why two young girls need to call each other "Miss."

You begin!

May the Lord grant you all that your heart desires.

And accept an embrace from

Chiara who remembers you so fondly.

---

3. St. Francis of Assisi.

Letter 4

Worldly Ambitions Are Too Petty

Letter of March 15, 1944 to Fosca Pellegrini

A couple of months after the "discovery" of Jesus Forsaken Chiara reveals the origins of her experience: An unending desire to love and an awareness of the fragileness of life. These were the first stepping stones in her ascent to God: The encounter with the source of Happiness. She signs: Silvia Clare.

March 15, 1944

Dearest Fosca,

I've just received your little letter in which you share with me a bit of your life.

I'm glad you were so open with me because I'm one of those who care about you.

Don't worry, dear Fosca, we're not the only ones to have had the privilege of overcoming suffering with joy! You'll do it too if you're willing to follow in the path of such a great ideal!

You're young like me, and that's why I don't hesitate to suggest this to you, because, so long as youth continues to smile upon us it will be easy for us to follow any path. But once age has set in, thoughts, inclinations, tendencies and personal ways of doing things — oh then it's nearly impossible to point life in the direction of an Ideal and give your all, all the energy of your spirit, toward its realization.

Fosca, there are two thoughts, or rather, two driving forces that give intonation to my life. And they satisfy this little heart of mine that is ever so restless until it rests in Something[4] where it can say: Here's what I tried so long to find. Finally, I've found it!

These two driving forces are:

---

4. The reference is to St. Augustine, *The Confessions* (1, 1).

9

1) An endless, overbearing, and ongoing desire to love.
2) A thought: Time flies at maddening speed. You only live once;
either you spend your life well or you spend it badly!

When that luminous moment of death (real life) will draw near, that moment which, in my Ideal, is more appealing than all others, then, looking back, before the big leap into Happiness (for which we all yearn either voluntarily or involuntarily) shall I be able to say: I lived by an Ideal, *the* Ideal, the most beautiful Ideal, the one that death doesn't snuff out but only magnifies?

Or will I have failed in life when I find myself confronted with a future that is totally unfamiliar to me, one I had never even imagined, one so far from my way of thinking that was always so stuck to this earth?

Even amid the occupations of everyday life, did I let my soul soar above everything, over the attachments — though always with and among the people — so high, so high, above, where my destiny lay?

Believe me, Focsa, such thoughts make me tremble and they encourage me to keep on going. They contain the leaven of my Ideal. And so I go on living, joyfully making use of everything in life, like so many stepping stones that help me to reach the heights there above!

Dear Fosca, you understand such things. You didn't suffer in vain. Perhaps in your pain you often asked the reason for so much suffering and very few were able to respond or provide the balm for your wounded soul.

You've certainly understood for yourself — since suffering is a light — that our heart will never, never, never be fully satisfied! Indeed, like me, you'll also have observed that in the world we move from one moment to the next constantly dissatisfied. We know that nothing can give us that happiness which we long for, yet we delude ourselves that we will find it "farther on." But when that "farther on" arrives, complete happiness is never there! Our life is a constant alternation between anxiety and relative peace — never a moment of pure joy!

Still our hearts cry out for it. They feel its strong attraction!

Why?

Look on high, to the Ideal, dear Fosca!

Put all your strength into it! At last you will find happiness.

Go through the world, but not like those who have eyes for only what is in the world. Move around here below, but never belong to here below!

Too petty are the ambitions of this world, a world that you too have experienced in that anguished heart of yours. Our soul was made to soar and most of the time we clog it down with our physical needs!

Will you join us and find out whether happiness exists? Write me again and often. I would like you to be happy as I am.

With my hand in yours for the ascent,

Silvia Chiara

A Fleeting Moment

An undated letter (1944?) to youths
of the Third Order

With its emphasis on concrete love for neighbor, this letter is certainly from the beginnings of Chiara's adventure. Her first response to God, whom she discovered as Love, was to help the poor and needy of Trent. Although she does not yet speak of unity, she emphasizes mutual assistance which leads to universal fraternity.

My Sisters!

From the Heavenly heights where he lives blest and anxious to see the completion of the work that God gave him to do, Francis — the saint of Fire and action — looks with saintly hopefulness upon us youths who are throbbing and blazing with life.

Listen to what a brother heart has to say!

Burst through every dam, every shadow, every difficulty, every narrow way of thinking and keep your eye on the Heaven that is there waiting for us with its endless reward.

We think too seldom of Heaven!

The task of bringing Heaven to earth and earth to Heaven lies with lively youths like us who are not yet attached to the things of this world! Earthly angels and Heavenly men! Keep watching for that prize which will soon be in our possession when we are alone with God!

Each of us will stand before Him then, to give an account of what she has gathered that is incorruptible and eternal.

Time is a flash and, in our hands, only the fleeting moment.

Plant it in God and as you go, accomplish works for Heaven!

Look around: All of us are brothers and sisters, no one excluded!

Beneath the individual features of each one of us we find the Christ who must grow in us: Christ Crucified and Forsaken beneath miserable and sin-ridden human remains.

Take heart: He's already overcome the world!

Let us see each other as God sees us, not to condemn and despair, but to be merciful to each other and to help one another.

Let us love each other! One day all of us will be together up there forever if we have had the courage here below to love without looking for excuses.

Let us be united for the same ideal: Universal fraternity in one Father, God, who is in Heaven.

Let's act: Let our love be truth and let it be deeds!

"Little children, let us love, not in word or speech, but in truth and action" (1 Jn 3:18).

Why are we afraid to say to everyone that we are only passing through here below and that there above we will be staying forever?

Why not enlighten our brothers' blindness, if we have the Light and if we are the Light?

Let's love with the truth!

Let's love with deeds!

As children of the Most High we were born and raised in the Mercy of God. Then let us be like our Father, "mercy alive," and let us do works of mercy.

How many brothers and sisters pass by us every day! In each of them Christ wants to be born, to grow, to live, and to resurrect. He asks us for help, comfort, advice, light, admonishment, bread, housing, clothing, and prayer...

Let's live the present moment and, in the present moment, the work of mercy that God is asking of us.

Only in this way will we be moving in the direction of Heaven.

Sr. Chiara

The Reason for My Life

April 16, 1944

A letter to Elena Molignoni, a girl from Castello di Ossana in Val di Sole where Chiara had been working as a school teacher in 1938–39. Encouraged by the parish priest, Father Francis Barcolla, Chiara started a Catholic Action group and young Elena attended.

In 1944, Chiara was enrolled in philosophy at the University of Venice but was unable to attend classes because of the war. The "hole" was the popular name given to the bomb shelter. This letter summarizes the yearning that filled Chiara's heart.

Third Sunday of April 1944
"Omnia mea tua sunt"[5]

Dearest Elena,

I take advantage of an air raid alarm to answer your letter. I'm sit-

---

5. All that is mine is yours (Jn 17:10).

ting here in a meadow next to the shelter, waiting to enter the hole when the bombers arrive.

What you wrote gave me pleasure, such pleasure that I felt that our hearts were beating as one.

You ask me what I'm doing. It's hard to put it into writing, but if I could say in just a few words the reason for my life, I would have to say: I love God and I would like to love Him as He has never been loved before. I work to make Him be loved.

Then there are my studies. I'm in my first year at the University of Venice, but studies aren't my purpose in life.

In life, in unity, that would be such a small thing in front of a God who lifts up the lowly and brings down the mighty.[6] I study because it's God's will and the effort and fatigue are the penitential price I pay for souls.

Everything else that happens in my life doesn't touch me. I've only one desire, my passion, that Love be loved.[7]

I feel my powerlessness but surrender it to God. I base everything on a faith that can't crumble, because I believe in the Love of God. I believe that God loves me and, because of this Love, I ask great things of my life and of those who walk with me in my great Ideal, things worthy of people who know that they're loved by God...

Chiara

---

6. See Lk1:52.
7. Throughout these letters Chiara refers to God as "Love" (with a capital L). At times she uses the word to refer to the Godhead and at other times to refer to Jesus or to Jesus Forsaken.

I've Never Had Cause To Praise Life As I Have Now In This Hour

Letter of June 7, 1944 to Elena Molignoni

A few weeks before this letter was written, on May 13, 1944, the Lubich family's house at 1 Via Gocciadoro in Trent was badly damaged during a bombardment. The family fled from the city and headed for Centa, a mountain village in the province of Trent. Chiara stayed behind, alone in the city, to follow the young people whom she had drawn into her Ideal.

This detachment from her loved ones was a crucial step in her life because of the new life that emerged from this pruning. She makes mention in this letter of the horror of death following the bombardment of May 13th. Later she will describe how her brother, Gino, who was a medical student working at the city hospital, accompanied her through the ward where everyone had perished and, confronted by such a horrible sight he remarked: "Everything is vanity of vanities." It was a saying that would urge Chiara on in following Christ.

Elena later became a focolarina[8] and her brother, Giacomo, also entered one of the small communities known as the hearth (focolare). We don't know who the mother of Angel was, but he was most likely a boy who had recently died.

---

8. Focolarina and focolarino. A consecrated woman (focolarina) or man (focolarino) member of the Focolare Movement, who lives in community. Hearth (*focolare* in Italian) was the nickname given by others to the small community of women living a common life in the first community of Trent. It referred to the light and warmth that people found among them, which they attributed to the presence of Jesus among those who are gathered in his name (see Mt 18:20).

Dearest Elena,

Praise be to God that He wishes me to cling still to life, or praise be to God if tomorrow I am called to death! No, no, little Elena, whom I have so greatly loved, what you suggest is not the true life, this is not it at all. If the Lord will open the way to Eternity for me then I will praise Him, because then at last I shall be able to see Him.

Oh! my Elena, if only you were with me, I should be able to tell you all the things that I have seen.

I too have had the privilege of suffering with so many; I too have had my home damaged and rendered uninhabitable; I too have slept beneath the stars and walked miles on my feet; I too have suffered and wept, and for all this, Praise be to the good God that in His great love He has proved my love; Elena dear, I have never had cause to praise life as I have in this hour when I see that, *all things pass away* and all that remains is simply that love of God which we have gathered in our heart.

Oh, my Elena! Believe me! I want all that is good for you, believe me I have seen death in all its most pitiable conditions.

Oh, no, no, let us not cling too closely to anything because all dies; only God can light a fire in us which endures through life and all eternity, God who is Love! Yes, I love life because with it I prepare myself for death that is the *true resurrection*.

Down here there are always alarms and the roar of the engines! We are always awaiting the call from God. It is only an act of obedience which springs from my heart; obedience to the divine will!

Oh! Elena how much my divine crucified Jesus has taught me. It is true that I studied at the university, but no book, however beautiful or profound, has given such strength to my soul and above all such love, as has Jesus Crucified. Before Him every sorrow seems to me as nothing and I await sorrow, be it great or small, *as the greatest gift from God,* because by it there is proof of my love for Him.

My dear Elena, I pray you, and I would write this with my blood, love the Crucified! It's all there, all the gift of God: He cannot give us more than that. And when sorrow, great or small, strikes at your heart, cry out with me, Thank you, thank you, O Love Immense! Not only do I accept whatever You give me, but behold with total joy I offer You

16

all the love that this heart contains. Think Elena, *we are able to love God with this tiny heart!* We are able to love God! Nothing, nothing can take away this love, not even the worst bombardments!

Read often what in opening my heart to you I have written and if you hear no further news of me, simply pray to God for me, pray to Jesus crucified for love of me and to the Virgin Sorrowful Mother of the Fair Love. And may the Lord take everything else away from you and give you a great love, a love of fire, of flame. This and this only is my wish for all your companions and for the parish priest whom I ask you to greet on my behalf.

Greet Angelo's mother. Tell her that I carry him in my heart and I pray to him that from heaven he bless his mother.

Silvia

What news of Giacomo, your brother, and your cousin?

*L*etter 8

What You Are Searching For Exists!

A letter from June 1944 to some young members
of the Franciscan Third Order

Chiara had only recently been left alone in Trent and the Flame of God was burning in her heart more and more. She calls this month "the month of Flame" and, in this letter, she describes the endlessly diverse colors of this Love.

Little Sister in God's Immense Love!

Listen please to the voice of this little heart! You have been dazzled along with me by the flaming brightness of an ideal that surpasses and summarizes everything:

By God's Infinite Love!

Oh, my little sisters, it is your God and mine who has established between us a bond that is stronger than death and will never pass away. Like the spirit, it is endless, tenacious, sweet and immortal as God's Love!

Love joins us as sisters!

Love has called us to Love!

Love has spoken in the depths of our hearts, saying:

"Look around you. Everything in the world passes away. Each day comes to an end and evening drops so quickly. Each life has its sunset and soon the sunset of your life will be upon you! But never despair: Yes, yes, everything passes away, for nothing of what you see and love is destined to last forever! Everything passes away, leaving you with nothing but hopes and regrets!"

But don't despair: Your constant hope tells you: *"Yes, there is what you are looking for: There is that infinite and immortal longing, a hope that never ends, a faith that breaks through the darkness of death and is a light to those who believe; your hope is not in vain, your believing is not in vain. It's not in vain!"*

You hope, you believe — *because of Love.*

This is your future, your present and your past: It's all summarized in the word Love!

You've always loved. Life is a continuous seeking after loving desires that rise from the bottom of the heart! You've always loved! But you loved badly! You loved what dies and is vain, and only vanity was left in your heart. *Love what doesn't die! Love the One who is Love!* Love the One who in the evening of your life will look only at your tiny heart. You'll be alone with Him in that moment; terribly unhappy the one whose heart is filled with vanity, immensely happy the one whose heart is overflowing with the infinite Love of God!

My little sister, I beg you, listen to "time" as it rushes by, listen to those relentless heartbeats as they keep knocking against the door of your soul, as they continually and invitingly turn you toward *Love!*

9. June is traditionally the month of the Sacred Heart of Jesus.

Love, love, love! Love is our destiny![10]

Think about life that rushes by! Throw aside whatever's unworthy of you, of your heart, which is small, yes, but noble, precious, and powerful: *It can love God!* Why spoil it? On what?

Go through the world singing *to Love*.

Come along! Cover everything in a sea of Flame!

There's not a suffering in the world, a joy in the world, a feeling in the world that we cannot drown in God's love!

Yes there is suffering in the world, but for those who love suffering is nothing, even martyrdom is a song! Even the Cross is a song. The Lord God is Love! And suffering is the fierce test of Love, its undeniable divine seal.

Up! Up! Come along with me! Let's go to Love! Let's run to Love!

That's right: Let us not allow anything painful to pass by us in life without accepting it and desiring it in order to prove to God who is immense Love, our own small but tenacious love!

Let us allow our hearts only one need: the need to love.

Let us allow our minds only one need: constantly to confront every thought with the infinite and endless love of God.

May the Lord God give you Love — a Love of Flame and of Light.

Sister Chiara

---

10. The first three "loves" are verbs. The first sentence is in the imperative form.

Part 2

"For I decided to know nothing
among you except Jesus Christ,
and him crucified"

(1 Corinthians 2:2).

Letter 9

At the Service of God's Plans

Advent 1944, Letter to Lolanda Calderari

A few years older than Chiara, Lolanda was a social worker of the Red Cross. She lived in Piazza Cappuccini near to the home where Chiara had moved in September 1944. Chiara indicates Saint Catherine of Siena to her as a model, who was very popular in Italy at this time because of her spirituality centered on Blood and Fire. We perceive that Chiara has begun to be conscious of the fact that she is the bearer of a special gift from God and that she has been chosen by Jesus to be his confidant concerning his wound (Letter 14). The word "key" (Letter 14) appears indicating that the Cross, especially Jesus Forsaken, unlocks every heart and leads it to holiness.

In the Advent of Love's Reign!

Dearest Lolanda,

I left you first, and as soon as I did, I abandoned you to Love that He might make you into a Saint Catherine for today.

I went to St. Mark's and I prayed to Him, the Almighty, for you.

I was so close to Him with body and with heart and He spoke to me of you. He told me that your desire has been accepted in Heaven and that He, the Almighty, is ready for it to be implemented.

However, he told me to say this to you:

The desire to be like Saint Catherine is a good thing.

The possibility of being another Saint Catherine depends all on God and all on you. Everything depends on your will being *the* Will.[11]

Lolanda, everything depends not on your heart aspiring to be Saint

---

11. The will of God.

Catherine, but on your heart aspiring to love more than Saint Catherine did.

Yes, Lolanda, Love told me that if you would like, you can do more than Saint Catherine did, because the power that He offers to you is more than what He gave to her.

"Never," He said, "does the Almighty make duplicates. And you should not only aspire to do great things, but *excelling* things." (Almighty as He is, He can share His Omnipotence with us.)

He said that externals which make such an impression on the world of then and of now and that made everyone call Catherine "the saint," count for nothing, for they're only the outward expressions of the passion that was burning deep inside her.

It is we who are only used to judge and let ourselves be dazzled by the exterior.

But the Lord God sees into hearts and the saints know what has value:

love.

Catherine did what she did without being aware of it; otherwise, she wouldn't have been holy.[12]

She was aware and had knowledge of only one thing:

Jesus Crucified,

the Truth, the Almighty, the Absolute Love!

She was literally in love with this Divine Man and her heart was locked into a Divine Madness of Love for this Crucifix that only she understood in those days.

Absorbed by this divine passion, fed on His Most Sweet Blood, she understood *nothing else* but Him, and she could see nothing else but Him!

There it is, Lolanda.

Nothing but this Love which can be born in your heart too (and God wants it to be), can bring you to what you want and to what He wanted from you even before you did.

Believe me, Lolanda, *Love* is going to be the salvation of the 20th century because *Love* is God.

All the more or less secular traps are a waste of time or perhaps they serve as the subsoil for God's plans.

---

12. Chiara is probably referring to the unusual spiritual and mystical phenomena that surrounded Catherine.

Fill yourself, then, with this personal Love for the God Man, the only one who is truly worthy of love.

But you don't know what a fortune is hanging over you, you don't know.

Maybe now Love will accomplish the miracle of making you understand what my heart has understood through contact with Him who is my Only Love!

I told you: Love doesn't repeat itself. When Love reappears in the world it will be new and of such a brilliant clarity that it will surpass by an infinite measure what has ever been seen until now.

And Love *has* reappeared in the world and given to our hearts the *Key* that opens *every* heart.

Believe it, Lolanda, everyone who rose to holiness was given a more or less lofty place relative to the amount of intensity with which they *loved Jesus Crucified!*

And so: Do what I want to do: Plunge yourself, body and soul, *into the Abandoned Love!*

You have heart and understanding. Listen:

Think of the infinite difference between the pain of Jesus — who was crucified by His *enemies*, abandoned by His disciples, forced to entrust His Mother to another — and the immense pain of feeling disunited from his Father whom he loved as Himself and with whom he formed a single oneness.

Think: It was that atrocious doubt of no longer being one with the Father that made Him come out with that cry:

"My God, my God why have you abandoned me?"

This Cry should break the heart of every man, for everyone has been made by this divine anguish worthy of being *joined* to God, *united* to God as an adopted son!

Here! Here! Here lies the *Immensity of Love!* He gives us His Divinity.

Just think, Lolanda, you who have so much heart, think of this Jesus hanging there like a rag, His soul torn by grief, *doubting that He's still God!*

Think of it and allow Him to rest upon that heart of yours that desires great things,

But for Him!

Tell Him to abandon upon you His Divine Humanity which has

been reduced to nothing in order to give us Everything, reduced to hatred (because he almost believed that the Father no longer loved him) to give us Love — tell Him to abandon it upon you and to tell you all about His torment so that you, enflamed and nearly mad for so much love, may run through the world, not with your own little heart, but with the heart of God; burned by Love, so that you will not be able to touch anything without setting it ablaze, and chase after the abandoned Lord of hearts.

Swear to Him, assure Him with your life that He is God precisely because, out of Love, He desired to stay in doubt for that moment! Swear to Him that your heart will never again abandon Him, so that He can always find in your heart the paradise that He lost when it seemed His Father had turned his eyes away. And then do whatever you want, for it will all be great in the eyes of God and of the world.

Decide to follow and love, Love Crucified, this way, *in his greatest pain*, the *expression of the greatest Love*!

In answer to your proposal to Love, Love-Almighty, who will never be outdone in generosity, will have even greater designs on you than those that He had for Saint Catherine, because Love is inexhaustible and never stops casting its Fire into the world, Fire which he had reserved for everyone but which no one wanted.

You open your whole heart to Him and say that He should give to you such a force of Love, as much as he was keeping in store for everyone in the world today.

Tell Him that your only passion is *Him crucified in His abandonment!*

Only then will you set fire to Italy![13] Oh! No, it's not enough just to preach honesty with our lips and with our lives. The Lord God must preach *from* our hearts with all his Love!

I *invoke* upon you from this Abandoned Jesus who confided his Spiritual Wound to me, which had the power to incinerate the heart (the Wound of the Abandonment), His Omnipotent Blessing that He may never allow you to have peace until you give yourself over to this madness of Love!

My God-Love has a right to hearts that burn with love and He

---

13. An allusion to Saint Catherine who said: "If you are what you should be, you'll set fire everywhere in Italy" (Letter 261 to Stefano di Corrado Maconi).

expects everything of your heart, all the power that He has instilled within it (the power of Love).

Lolanda, don't put on the brakes and with that generosity that blossoms so easily within you, place yourself at the disposal of God's Plans. Be of strong purpose; let it be like an oath that you will never stray from seeing that love is never abandoned by you nor by anyone else.

But you will never be able to do anything unless you sincerely love Him and don't spare anything in Love.

Lolanda, it's Love who told me to write you in this way. How much God loves you, my little Lolanda!

Your Silvia

 **L**etter **10**

Help Me to Comfort Him

Undated letter (Autumn 1944?)
to her sister, Liliana

The date of 1944 is probable because Chiara speaks of the "little house," a name given, in honor of Loreto, to the small apartment at Piazza Cappuccini where Chiara had moved with some companions in September 1944. This little house was the first "hearth."

Chiara writes to her younger sister for whom she felt much tenderness and love. She felt understood by her sister. She doesn't hesitate to entrust to her the "great mission" to which she herself feels called, almost desiring to share the burden with her.

Liliana was called by various diminutives (Liana, Jenny, Janney).

Dearest Liana,

You departed from the little house leaving in my heart the fragrance of your quiet kindness that is truly beginning to blossom. I give glory to my Love!

Janney of my heart! See, I always want you near, but you already know it. Accept the Divine Will and since you love me so well, pray often for me. I feel in my heart such a noble mission, but my misery and inability weigh me down.

I want to make Love to be loved, especially and above all, by you who are my sister by blood and by the Ideal. Janney, forget everything, but never forget Jesus. You know that I gave Him all of my life, miserable and poor, yes, but all, all that I had.

I can already see Him on that day when He will be judging me and asking me for an account of my Ideal! Oh! Then I would like to hear Him say: *"Come Chiara, my little spouse. You were unfaithful at times, but you tried to instill love for me in people's hearts. Come, I offer you my kiss, God's kiss!"*

Yes, Liana, with others I can't say everything because they'll think I'm out of my mind, but you're my sister and you know that I have my head on straight. You also know the tabernacles in the churches, you've seen the loneliness and abandonment of Jesus. It pains me! You see, Liana, He's my Spouse, He's my God, He's my Jesus, Savior, brother, friend, comfort — my everything!

Help me to comfort Him! Go to Him, even if it costs you! Send him your heart when you're at home. Talk to Him, speak to Him, speak to Him! You're a quiet person and that's fine! Then let all of your silence be for God! Look at Him on the cross and love Him to madness.

Teach everyone to love Him. Support Carla all the way. Do my part in defending her. Be patient with her so that she can be good. Let her follow her own way. I send you a big, big, big kiss.

Your, Silvia

Letter 11

The Place of Honor

Undated letter (November 1944?)
to Rosetta Zanoni

Rosetta was a young woman from Trent who fled with her family to Calceranica, a village in Valsugana at the foot of the Italian Alps. She had met Valeria and Angelelli (here called Angelina) Ronchetti, from Pergine. She travelled every day by truck down to the center of town and returned on the evening train. During these very uncomfortable trips, in the cold that she suffered on the truck (see Letter 15) she caught pleurisy and was hospitalized. Chiara writes to Rosetta when she is ill, helping her to understand the preciousness of the moment.

1944

Dear Rosetta,

I hardly know you by sight, but my heart already knows so much about you. Only two things I know, but they are everything for me:

That you've been called by a secret voice, silent and sweet: the Voice of *Love*.

That Love has thought of great things for you and has turned a *privileged glance* in your direction.

These two things I believe with *steadfast faith in Love* and this allows me to understand you with that knowledge that is love.

Dear little Rosetta, how great is the gift that Love has given to you. Think of it: He gives His gifts in proportion to the Love that He has for souls and He suggests to their hearts thoughts that are only sweet and divine.

Think of it, Rosetta, the Lord God came to earth only once, and that once as a *man and He let Himself be put on the cross!*

This thought gives me strength and joy to accept the small crosses that always seem to follow us.

But when He gives to the souls that He loves — *like yours that's been touched by Love* — even greater sufferings, *it's because He wants His Love to triumph in you completely!*

Rosetta, yesterday Angelina mentioned your name and as I thought of you, I said to myself: "What a great fortune has befallen her." A patient who does not know Love is unfortunate because, as the Lord says in the *Imitation of Christ*, "It's so difficult to make progress in Love when one is ill."[14]

Oh! I beg you with all my heart: Don't let even a moment of your precious life be lost by spending it in vain.

But someone who *knows Love and unites her sufferings to the sufferings of Jesus on the Cross, losing her single drop* of blood in that Ocean of Blood of the Divine Blood of Christ, has the *highest place of honor that a person can have*:

To be like God come into the world: Redeemer of the world.

Rosetta, you're *with us*: Your love for the Lord is all one with ours.

You know? Oh! Yes you know! Jesus converted the world with the word, example, and preaching, but He transformed it *with proven Love*: the Cross. Up there for two and a half hours in a state of such tremendous anguish and horrendous pain He drew our hearts to Him.

Believe me, Rosetta: One minute of your[15] life spent on those white bed sheets is worth far more than all the activism of a preacher who talks and talks but loves God little. You love Him in this way: "So be it, O Lord, and even more if You wish, as long as You are loved! I know that I don't suffer much, but I join my small sufferings to Yours which is Immense! Thus you will make Love be loved again."

I'm close to you with my heart and wish you well.

Silvia

I'd be so glad if you wrote to me.

---

14. A liberal translation of the *Imitation of Christ*: "You can do many good works when in good health; what can you do when you are ill? Few are made better by sickness. Likewise they who undertake many pilgrimages seldom become holy" (chapter 23).

15. Chiara underscores this word three times.

L*etter* 12

Your Good Fortune And Ours

Letter of December 8, 1944
to Rosetta Chiara Zanoni

Chiara alludes to suffering that is overcome by joy. She has become aware that God has given a special gift to her. She calls Jesus Forsaken "the new wound" and the Ideal that she proposes has become the "rule" for a new life. Alda is Alda Ghezzi, one of the young women who followed Chiara.

Feast of the Immaculate Conception, 1944

Dearest Rosetta,

I've wanted to write you for some time and now the chance has come. I know from Alda and Angelina how much you love Love.

Little Rosellina of Love, the Lord God is so great, Love is so much *Love*!

You are also with us. Your Love is also abandoned. Yes, yes, you also know that we need to comfort and console Him completely! Do you know Jesus Forsaken? Do you know that He's given us everything? What more could a god give to us out of Love than to forget that He is God?

Those of us who follow with you this most beautiful and appealing Ideal, have thrown our whole soul into the new wound of the Abandonment! And in there we are safe because we live in the Heart of our Love. Not only that, but from within that wound we can see the entire Immenseness of God's Love poured out over the world.

Place yourself inside too! You'll have the Light of Love, because Jesus is the Light of the world.

You don't know your good fortune — and ours — at being able to follow this Abandoned Love!

In His inscrutable plans He's chosen us from among thousands and thousands of others, to hear His anguished Cry: *"My God, my God why have you abandoned me?"* And, as God, He's made this Cry into the Rule of a new life to be lived in a new calling.

Our Love, the Love that should reign in our hearts, *must be Heavenly Love, Love forever joyful,* because that's how Jesus wants it to be.

Believe me, Rosetta, that for all the sufferings that Love sends us, *it's all nothing compared to the Ideal that no other can surpass.*

Therefore, let us not offend this Love with our melancholy and complaining, but let us be ever ready to overcome every pain with joy and in joy because this is God's will for us, and we have all the Grace we need, we just have to know how to make use of it.

May the Immaculate take you beneath Her Mantle which is more dazzling than the sun, by allowing you to live the Ideal in all its fullness.

Chiara,
who, in Love, loves you as herself.

Our sisters here are greeting you with all their hearts.

He Distributes Only Love

Letter of Christmas 1944
to Pierita Folgheraiter

Pierita had been one of Chiara's colleagues during the 1940 –41 school year at the Capuchin Orphanage in Cognola,

Trent. She was also Chiara's friend.
In the name of their friendship, Chiara shares with Pierita
the loving passion that is invading her heart: that Love be loved.
She calls her friend both Pierina and Pierinetta.

Christmas, 1944

Dearest Pierina,

... your letter arrived with the Christmas wishes from your good heart.

Oh, my little Pierinetta, how I'd like to have you near to me in this time of hard and bitter struggle: *but also of so much Light and Fire and Warmth!* You know what's happened to me exteriorly, you're up to date on my sufferings which have certainly opened my heart to an under- standing of what Humanity suffers; but you don't know, you don't know what the suffering has given to me.

Pierinetta you've always been a trusted friend who has been out of touch for so long, but when she reappears is *more alive than ever in her affection and remembrance.*

You know: Jesus, my Jesus and yours has made me suffer.

And I have suffered! But he is not a distributor of pain! No, no! He always *permits* but never sends the suffering that *people* always obtain for themselves. He distributes *only Love!*

No one knows *how to love like Him! No one knows how to console like Him!*

He's infused a great Passion within my heart: Jesus Crucified and Abandoned!

From high on the Cross he says to me: "... I let all that I was fade away ... all of it! I'm no longer beautiful; no longer strong; I have no peace; justice has disappeared; science is unknowing; truth has van- ished. All that is left is my Love, which longs to give away my Godly wealth *for you...*"

This is what He says to me and He calls me with his "mad" Love for me, to follow Him "mad" with Love!

He is my Passion, which I've confided to you, Pierina, that you might keep it buried in the secrecy of your heart. You wouldn't betray your friend!

Therefore, in the name of the One Crucified by Love for me and *for you*, I dare you to accept my longing and make it your own.

May Love make you appreciate how much He loved you and how

much He loves you. And may He give rise to my Passion of Love within your heart, so that He may finally find in you a heart here on earth with a bit of that consolation which the world refuses to give Him.

Silvia

Letter 14

Would You Make the Flame In My Heart Your Own?

Letter of December 1944 to her mother

References to the war and the impracticality of reaching her parents where they are staying — this letter from the "Christmas of Love's New Reign" must be from 1944 (see letter 10 from the "Advent of Love's New Reign"). Chiara names each of her sisters and her brother.

When she writes that she was "called to live where there is danger and need" she is referring to the promise she made to stay in the city, which occurred on May 13, 1944 (see letter 7). The letter was written a year after her vow of perpetual virginity ("I've married Him").

The fire within her burns with such strength that she doesn't hesitate to communicate it to her mother. Indeed, she totally engages her mother in her Ideal, describing it to her with enthusiasm, for she is certain that no one more than her mother would understand. And yet, she signs her letter "with a heart that perhaps, as yet, you don't know..."

In the Christmas of Love's New Reign
December 1944

Dearest Mommy,

It's been some days now since I've been living with anguish in my heart. When Daddy came he found that I had come down with a bit of the flu. The air-raid shelter is cold and the alarms are unrelenting. The cold on the truck is unbearable and fatal for such a fragile body as mine.

Reasoning it out, Daddy saw that it would be impossible to come at Christmas and it seems impossible to me too. I would need transportation. And that's always difficult to find. Christmas away from you makes me weep, Mom. I'm often taken by homesickness that only the Love of God can make me overcome.

I see him up there on the Cross suffering from homesickness too and the abandonment of the Father and it seems that he's bringing about in me what I so often ask of him: "Grant me to experience something of your Sufferings, especially a bit of your terrible abandonment, so that I can be closer and more similar to you who in your infinite Love have chosen me and taken me to be with you."

Then I feel that he consoles me saying to me that if I left everything only for love of him when he called me — including mother and father — if I chose to live where there is danger and need, then he will be my consolation! Then he places in my soul the Fire of Love which makes me want to cry: "Love is not loved!"

And this is the first thing that I call out to you, Mommy. At least you hear me. In the name of your love for me, for Gino, Daddy, Carla and Liliana, I beg you to hear me.

Don't think it folly what I ask of you, nor imagination. No, Mommy, believe me! Only one thing matters in this life which passes in a flash, and there is only one thing that we should ask of God: *to love him*. Mommy, believe me. You'll see when you're in Paradise — where I hope we will be together forever — you'll see that I was correct.

In your own life you married Daddy and you loved your children. You also loved God. But now, the Lord, through me, me, such an insignificant thing (you know me), tells you, Mommy, that what mat-ters is to love God!

Believe it, Mommy. Jesus died for you and being God he would have died for your salvation alone had it been necessary! Look at him there where he is crucified and think: What if it had been your son? Listen to him cry: "*My God, my God, why have you abandoned me?*"

This is a cry that repeats itself at every moment in my heart. Think of him nearly desperate and dying and pierced like a lamb! Poor Jesus! Come now, Mommy, tell me that you love him too and that you want to make others love him! Tell me that if your Sylvia had to die before you, you would take as your own the Flame that burns in her heart. I've touched upon this world too, Mommy, and I've found hearts that were more or less noble, but no one have I found who loves me as much as He. In Heaven you will know how much he's forgiven me as well as the marvels he performs in me and in the young women who follow in my way, the way of Love.

Don't tell anything to anyone, Mommy! I've married him and I've tried to extinguish every other desire outside of him. He and his cry of abandonment have swept me away, Mom, made me pass beyond everything as my heart is crushed. Yes, Mommy, only he could have done it. He doesn't neglect our feelings but makes us experience them in the deepest depths of our heart and then he makes us go beyond them because he is omnipotent, he's God. And now Christmas comes and my heart caves in at the thought of being away from you. If you could … come down, Mommy.

But now the danger is furious and rising as the alarms never stop and we're taking refuge in our houses. And it pains me to think of you always in the shelter. Today Daddy is at Gino's, then he'll come back and we'll see. In case it doesn't work out it will be good for Carla and Liliana to be with you on that day and for me and Ginetto it will be another occasion to offer a new sacrifice to Love.

Yes, yes, anything, even death, as long as Jesus who loved us so much as to die for us is loved by all people, as long as consolation rises for him and peace in the hearts of those who don't have any expectations but to love Love! You'll see, Mommy, how all the rest will be given to you as well when we seek only his Reign! And what is his Reign if not telling everyone to love the Lord God and to love each other?

Share my passion for Love, Mommy, and since you know how to express things in words so well, spread it to everyone. Believe me when I tell you that Jesus is expecting that your heart love him in this way as

Saint Rita loved him, and she was also a mother! Write to me regarding this. This is the only thing that matters. Believe me!

Oh! if only the Holy Infant would bring my passion to your heart! I think he will certainly have a special blessing for the mother of such a miserable daughter, even insolent, but whom he has chosen for his bride, so that it will be more obvious that He is at work.

With a heart that perhaps, as yet, you don't know, Mommy,

I kiss you goodbye,

Silvia.

A Great Mission

Letter of January 1, 1945 to her sister, Lilliana

Chiara encourages her sister who is anxious over Paolo, her fiancé, who is at the battlefront, and Chiara is able to be so reassuring because she trusts in God. She signs the letter, "Lila" which is the diminutive of "Silvia." This letter shows once again how Chiara's view of things is founded on unity first and then distinction, on the Christian vocation which is a participation in the passion, death, and resurrection of Christ. She tells her sister: "You espouse Love Crucified and Abandoned as I do."

New Year's 1945

My Little Janney,

This day went by in Love too, though the "hawks" tried to turn things cruel and ugly.[16] I finally left the air-raid shelter after being inside for six hours. It wasn't cold and my heart was full of Jesus For-

---

16. "Hawks" refers to the bomber planes.

saken for Whom I live and suffer all these small pains that he gives me so that

He may no longer be abandoned!

My little Janney, you see that I am living far away from you and how now more than ever I would so much want to share life with you in sisterly affection and comfort.

But you know, my Janney, you know that my Love has called me to fulfill a great mission.

I have to, I want to make Him loved by the whole world, because He was left crucified and abandoned for me.

And you, Liliana, who love me, you whom I saw growing in Love by my side — even if you are so far away but abandoned to Love:

Have pity for this Jesus, who continues to knock at your heart for a bit of consolation from you!

You should, you must embrace my Ideal! Even if your way is slightly different from mine. You can't get married as other girls of this world do! No, no! You won't espouse Paolo as a man. No, you'll espouse
Love Crucified and Abandoned,
like me!

How?

When Paolo returns (and he will surely return) you'll see the expression of God's Will in him. In his voice you'll hear the Voice of Jesus which says to you: "Tie your life to mine so that in our family I will never again be abandoned."

Like that, my Janney! Like that! See what wonders Love makes me say *for you*? See? I suffered thinking that you were going to embrace an ideal in life that was inferior to mine...

And the Lord who loves me, said to me: "Don't you realize that exterior acts like getting married to someone, doesn't matter at all and that the only thing that matters is the heart? I also love Liliana in the same way that I love you and I also abandon myself to her tiny little heart so that she will never have to abandon me!"

This is what Jesus said to me and this is what I say to you on this first day of the New Year! I hope, my Janney, that this year brings all Love to you and, as a great gift of Love to you, your darling Paolo.

Yours,

Lila

Letter 16

The Only Treasure I Possess

Letter of January 9, 1945
to her sister Liliana and Chiarella

*Chiarella was probably one of the young women who
belonged to the group that formed around Chiara, whom she
called "sisters."*

January 9, 1945

My Dearest Little Sisters,

I've waited for you in vain. You know why.

I send you these pages! Oh! How I want to hope that the momentum of your love for Jesus hasn't diminished! Is it true? Chiarella? Is it true, Janney? Woe to me if I heard you say that you've become lukewarm and don't love Him who is everything for us! *You haven't abandoned Him, have you?* I had hoped so much to console Love with both your hearts that it would be torment for me to see you slip back into your life as it was before.

And so I'll continue to write to you, to speak to you of Him. Read these pages. I've written them especially for you. But don't show them to anyone till I tell you to. Here the storm is rumbling all around us; always the same! But for your little sister who stays here only because of Him, because of Jesus Forsaken, because of the souls entrusted to me, a single glance at the Cross is all it takes! I see His Blood! I listen to His Cry!

I know that souls here are abandoned and that everyone is escaping. But I don't want to lose any souls. Jesus paid for them with His Blood.

I can very well offer up to Him a bit of the nostalgia I have for all of you, for Mom, and the effort in facing the difficult times that lie ahead. Always pray for me, my little sisters! Pray that I become a saint and, if the Lord wants, that I go on living in order to make Him be loved! Death doesn't frighten me: I've loved my Love and He alone will judge me. Stay faithful to Him always and receive from my heart the only treasure I possess: An endless desire to love Him as He has never been loved before!

Your Lila

Tell Me If He Didn't Love You

Letter of January 11, 1945
to her sister, Lilliana

She addresses her sister with the usual diminutive forms and Chiara herself signs her name with the diminutive. In this letter shines the human person's highest calling, to be God's "partner" in love.

Trent, January 11, 1945

My Dearest Janney,

Your letter and what you said gave me enormous pleasure, but especially your desire.

Oh! My Janney! I would like to be next to you, to take you by the arm to that little church up there, to draw you near to the Tabernacle and show you a double spectacle:

Below, a cold, bleak Tabernacle surrounded by flowers and candles, but *devoid of hearts;*

and inside:

The Living Jesus! Jesus who is God! He created you, He gave you the beauties of nature, love in the heart for Mom, Dad, Paolo, Silvia, Gino, Carla and all the people whom you love!

I would like to bring you there, near to that Jesus who will one day be your Paradise for all eternity and now calls you with his persistent Love. This Jesus, gone mad with love for these human creatures (you and I included), now desires, after dying in such a way, to perpetuate his sorrowful abandonment in the Tabernacle!

There in front of Him I would like to say to you:

"Tell me, Liliana, how could you not understand his Love? How could you not see Him abandoned when the church is so empty or filled only by greedy people that would rather ask him for all manner of things for themselves, everything that serves them in this life which passes by so quickly — rather than for Love, which is the only thing that has value.

Then I would tell you: Look higher to the Cross with Him on it!

Tell me if he didn't love you! Tell me what he must have felt when, without expecting it, he was abandoned by all, *there,* as he waited to die, under such sorrowful conditions, no longer looked upon even by his Father!

And all to wrench from your heart one act of Love! A bit of Love for Him!

Oh! Liliana, give all of your life to Him. Give Him your will. That's it: His entire Will must become yours. And His Will lies totally in this:

Love the Lord God with all your heart!

Love your neighbor as yourself.

Your neighbor (= the one closest to you) is the one with whom you will share your life. It's Paolo: Love him because Jesus gave him to you, and keep in mind that his soul is worth that immense suffering of Jesus Forsaken!

Love Him, therefore, as if he were Jesus Forsaken!

For Jesus Forsaken, pray, pray, pray that Paolo will realize that the only thing that has value is the Lord God who is Love and that he should run along with you preparing for the other life where purity arrives. My Lianella! Love Jesus in the Tabernacle: Tell Him that you want only to love Him and that Paolo would love Him. Actually — it's really Jesus who is suggesting this idea to me — tell Jesus, tomorrow morning at Holy Communion, that you offer *all your life to* Him with its toils, joys, and pains — but above all, its "effort" to become Flame, so that Jesus will be loved by Paolo and that Paolo may come to know Love! You'll see, you'll see, my Janney, what Love will do!

I abandon you to Him.

Your Lila

Believe, believe in Love: If He gave everything for you, then He forgave everything, from the moment he saw your disappointment. Chase away the scruples. Don't you believe that Jesus is capable of forgiving you when he was left abandoned on the cross for you?

L*etter* **18**

Rest in Humility If You Want to Love

Undated letter (perhaps early 1945)
to Vittoria Salizzoni

On January 7, 1945, Chiara named Vittoria "Little Wing" (Aletta). This word signified taking "flight," a word that they preferred to use instead of "vows," for it suggested a change in the way they lived: You used your "wings" and found yourself in a different dimension, in God, in the Ideal. As Father Casimiro heard Chiara give this name, he remarked: "Little Wing of Jesus Forsaken ... for she must take wing and fly to the wound of the abandoned Jesus to be his paradise!"

This letter speaks of a virtue that is always implied by Chiara, but rarely explained: humility.

Little Wing of the Abandoned Love!

Oh, my dear sister, how gladly I write to you, knowing that you've taken up the path to Jesus, to Love!

Look at Him, then, on the bloody cross as He emits that atrocious cry. You know that cry, for it is your life!

"My God, my God, why have you abandoned me?" and underneath He is asking you, "Little Wing, will you abandon me?"

Let us answer Him together: "Never! I would rather die."

My little sister, never abandoning Love means: to love Him, to possess Love!

And do you know the necessary condition for never abandoning Him ever, for being without fear of ever losing Him?

Hear what the saint says: *"There is nothing that can capture love as humility can."* [17]

This drew Him down from Heaven into the womb of the Blessed Virgin!

Humility triumphs in Jesus Forsaken who is the model of all the virtues; Jesus bears with the feeling of being unworthy of His Father's help.

And … after that cry the Father returns His love — and Jesus — "Into your hands, Father, I commend my Spirit." [18]

The saint continues: "There is no humility without love and no love without humility!" [19]

Love grows in a heart in proportion to the humility that is found there.

Always consider yourself the worst of all.

You don't know the weight of the graces that God has granted to you.

You, unlike many others, know the value of the abandonment. You know that there on the cross, he humiliated himself to such a point that those around him believed him to be not God, but merely a man.

And this was for your sake!

Rest in humility, little Wing, if you want to fly and to love! If your heart has proud and haughty thoughts, squeeze them out of you, before they become words!

Jesus judges you and He sees into the depths of your heart.

---

17. As in a game of chess when the "queen" captures the opponent's "king" in a checkmate. *"He will not be able to move out of our check, nor will He desire to do so."* (A sentence from St. Teresa of Avila in *The Way of Perfection*.) Teresa says that Our Lady's humility was the first to "capture" the King in the Virgin's womb.

18. Lk 23:46.

19. Chiara paraphrases St. Teresa of Avila who says: *"I cannot understand how humility exists, or can exist, without love, or love without humility…"* (*The Way of Perfection*, 16:2).

He *is* your heart.

I beg you, for the abandoned love, don't chase love away; rather, let humility grow in you so that He may fill you and you can be the Wing of his little paradise on earth.

Let's commend each other to Love.

Your sister, Chiara

What a Crowd Of Saints

A letter from 1945 (before April 25)
to Vittoria Salizzoni

Against a backdrop of insecurity which was highlighted by the war, and the dazzling brightness of God's light that shows up all our pettiness, Chiara finds a way forward in a more pure love for Jesus Forsaken, with the help of Saint Paul.

Little Wing of the Abandoned Love,

I heard again today about lives cut short in their prime. It's the Lord God who summons hearts.

Little Wing, look at the reason for living!

Don't find yourself at Heaven's Door with anguish in your heart because you can't begin again.

You only live once, and only briefly at that...

Do you know the reason for life?

You live to love!

If the Lord leaves you with a breath here below, give it all for Him! Don't turn back!

Yesterday I was nostalgically thinking to myself of all the time lost, the sins, the omissions — all the ugliness there was.

And things became cloudy for you and for me.

But just yesterday such a vibrant new light opened my soul to hope. Saint Paul, the saint who put so much fire into our heart says: "Beloved, I do not consider that I have made it my own; but this one thing I do: forgetting what lies behind and straining forward to what lies ahead, I press on toward the goal for the prize of the heavenly call of God in Christ Jesus" (Phil 3:13–14). And these words are the Word of God, the Word of the Spirit of Love.

The same for us, my little sister!

Press on!

Let it be our cry!

Everything crumbles, everything fades away ... but only what is not eternal crumbles and falls!

Your soul is immortal! The word of God is eternal — of God, who for us is Love especially when he shows us the vanity of all things. Then it's forward for us too without ever looking back!

Thrusting ourselves into His Heart that He might close us within his Wound and we might view from there.

There is a Forsaken Jesus for us to console with our love and with souls.

I thought: Be missionaries and baptize thousands!!!

Jesus in our heart: Be that little Wing that you are and cast into thousands, and millions of hearts the endless desire to love Love more than He could be loved by all the hearts in the world!

What a crowd of saints!

What a Paradise on earth for the Abandoned Love!

Forward!

May the Blessed Virgin change our willingness into reality!

Sister Chiara

ℒℯ𝓉𝓉ℯ𝓇 20

The Fullness of Joy

Letter close to Easter 1945
to an unknown recipient

The end of Lent and the Easter of 1945 marked an important stage in the life of Chiara and her companions. There is a quantum leap, as documented by the letters of that period (this and Numbers 22, 23, 24), an experience of joy, the transition to a totally new life. This letter highlights the necessary foundation for achieving this goal: Believing that God loves us and loving Him in return.

Easter 1945

My Dearest Little Sister in Saint Francis,

I just read this:

Saint Matilda saw the Lord open the Wound of His most sweet Heart and say: "Admire the size of my heart that you may know it well; nowhere more explicitly than in the words of the Gospel will you find Love, for never will you find expressed anywhere in words a love that is stronger or more tender: As the Father has loved me, so I love you."[20]

Perhaps you didn't always think that you were so precious a thing, the very object of God's love. But He loved you, even before you were born, and soon you will be returning to him. Time is like a flight, a very quick Passage.

The Resurrection draws near.

My heart would desire so much from you, being so aware of your worth. There's not enough gold in the universe that could pay for the value of your soul which has been purchased by the Blood of God.

---

20. St. Matilda von Hackenborn (1241–1299), Benedictine nun and mystic who received revelations concerning the love of Jesus and his Sacred Heart.

But if I could put into a few words what I'd like to tell you ... Listen: Rise to a totally new life and believe that God loves you.

I assure you the fullness of joy here below and a life that's a constant alleluia.

Every true joy will be the fruit of the only two flowers that can perennially blossom in the garden of your soul:

The strong desire to be loved and to love.

Your tiny heart is a mystery of the love of God.

It sings only when it is loved by an Infinite Love and when it can love an Infinite Love.

The Infinite Love loves you. Believe in this.

Whether you love the Infinite Love who is God, I don't know; I only hope that you do, for your own happiness.

During this Easter pass over to a continual giving of Love.[21]

May my wish for you come true.

Chiara

Desire From On High

Letter of April 3 or April 4
to Fosca Pellegrini
This period in Chiara's life was characterized by a new knowledge of God, as she clearly says: "only now do I know."

---

21. The Italian word for Easter is pasqua which means Passover.

Dear little Fosca,

Today, by a fortunate chance, I found an envelope, this envelope with your address on it.

For some time now, I haven't had any news from you. Current events have interrupted our correspondence.

I thought of you just a few days ago when Easter had already passed and all of us friends and sisters in the Ideal received from the Lord, the fullness of Joy!

I thought:

When I first met Fosca, I had already formed in my heart the idea that one day, by following our Ideal, I would bring her to complete happiness. I had noticed the strong momentums in her toward an Ideal that isn't deceptive, that doesn't disillusion, but leaves the soul with the fullness it's always been longing for.

That's what I thought.

How I would wish to have you near me now and talk to you and talk to you.

I'd tell you of the greatness of God's Love.

I'd speak words to you that before I didn't know and was only able to just barely make out, but only now I know well.

Write me some news.

Tell me how you're doing.

Tell me if you remember us, if you still have that great longing for what is On High!

I abandon you to Love.

Chiara

Letter 22

The Lord Loves As God

Letter from around 10–12 April 1945
to Fosca Pellegrini

During this Easter period Chiara continues with her companions to experience such joy that she would like to share it with everyone. This joy finds its origin in Jesus Forsaken.

Eastertide 1945

Little Heart Called to Love,

Let me talk to you today.

I'm with you in God's great Love.

You've seen the Way and had a glimpse of the prize. But perhaps you don't know the "roses" he uses to fragrance the course. Perhaps you don't know because you're still too far from the King of your heart who calls and waits, you still haven't known the effects of His Love.

Believe me when I tell you that there are full and overflowing riches awaiting you.

The Pascha has passed. The "passing over" took place for many among us. And it was a "passing over" of the endlessly loving Jesus who has left in our hearts the mark of God: A joy that knows no sunset.

In our first meetings when we limped because of the climb, it was already normal thinking that for those who followed Love and were able to say with sincerity: *"Omnia mea, tua sunt"* (all that is mine is yours), Paradise had already begun here below.

Now we no longer think it. We know it.

The Lord loves as God.

You don't know how thirsty I am to give to you all that God has given me.

I feel the words of the Apostle as my own: *"Sicut Dominus donavit vobis ita et vos."*[22]

Yes! The same for me!

I know that everything is great when our Love is great, even a glass of water given in His Name.

But among all the great and divine actions of a life spent in love, one is perhaps more divine: To give the fullness of joy to someone's heart.

This is what we want to learn how to give.

But you can't give what you don't have.

We're united, my little sisters. Because of the youngness of our age and our immaturity in Love we require a mutual bond of Love.

In God we can do all things.

In God we can do all things. Even the most daring flights are reserved for hearts that live by faith in a god who is God, Love, Omnipotent.

This I know: Jesus Crucified and Abandoned has granted Salvation and Holiness to the hearts of those who give everything to Him.

In that Heart,

Chiara

He'll Give You Everything

Letter of April 15, 1945
to Fosca Pellegrini

This letter was sent together with the preceding one and it picks up from the last sentence. Referring once again to the light of Easter, Chiara continues to describe an exchange of gifts between God and us.

---

22. "Forgive as the Lord forgave you" (Col 3:14).

Little heart that's been called to Love,

I only know that Jesus Crucified and Forsaken has granted Salvation and Holiness to hearts who give everything to Him.

I just now received your letter in which a small soul which is like yours is asking me: "But tell me: how can you lose your soul?"

Perhaps this question has flashed through your mind.

If you or that other little heart had asked me this question earlier, the answer would have been different.

Easter has passed and with it the Light.

Omnia mea tua sunt[23] *(All that is mine is yours): That's all!*

This is the motto of our newborn life.

"All that is mine is yours."

Thus says the soul when it has lost everything (voluntarily renounced everything out of love) and wants to lose even its soul to find it again in God.

Here then is how we should implement this sentence that is the purest expression of Love: *Omnia mea, tua sunt.*

Our soul is either in joy or it is in sorrow.

When the soul doesn't sing, then something is occupying it and this something should immediately be given to God.

The suffering could be brought on by external things (and these are more easily overcome by souls who want to love Love); the sufferings could be within us (scruples, doubts, melancholy, temptations, emptiness, homesickness).

They all need to be given to God.

The quicker the giving, the sooner Love descends into our hearts.

But be careful: A giver cannot go on keeping for her, a gift that's been given away.

If you feel something, whatever it may be, which doesn't allow your soul to be at Peace then you need to give it over to Him with an effort that is equal to the size of the gift.

If you keep something for yourself, even just the thought of the gift, then you appropriate a treasure for yourself (a tiny treasure) that no longer belongs to you.

Only into the extreme poverty of a soul which loses itself for love

---

23. See Jn 17:10.

does the Lord God enter triumphant with the fullness of joy.

That is why this Pascha was a "passing over" for all of us to a life of never-ending joy as we live the Ideal in its fullness.

Now, do you want the Eternal Model?

Jesus Crucified and Forsaken.

His soul, which is the soul of the God-Man, filled with the greatest suffering ever known in Heaven and on earth, the suffering of a God abandoned by God, never doubted for a moment about offering it to His Father: "*In manus tuas, Domine, commendo spiritum meum (Into your hands, Lord, I commend my spirit)*." [24]

Let it always be the same for us.

And do you know what Jesus will say in answer to your offer?

Omnia mea tua sunt (All that is mine is yours).

Everything He'll give you, the entire fullness of His joy

May He give you everything.

Chiara

Give, Give, Give…

Letter of April 22, 1945
to Fosca Pellegrini

In the enduring light of Easter, Chiara further expounds on the topic of "giving," a value which was dear to her throughout her life.

---

24. See Lk 23:46.

Little heart called to Love,

I want to share with you this latest development in our thinking so that the Light of Love will shine in you always more clearly.

Live the "omnia mea, tua sunt"[25] with growing perfection.

Believe it: This is our only possibility for advancing in the Way of Love.

And what is the special note of perfection for today?

It's this: that we always be quicker in giving to Him what is "ours."

What's mine?

All that concerns *me*, all that is not another's because it's *mine*, whatever pertains to me in particular: All of this "mine" *is his*.

Omnia mea, tua sunt.

So, in each moment, take all that's yours and give it to Him. Give it to Him always more immediately.

The quicker you give it to Him, the quicker you will be Him.

What could I tell you that would be greater than this? And what is a life in Love if not to live Him?

Herein lies our Holiness: To reach the point of becoming Him, of being able to say with Saint Paul: *"It is no longer I who live, but Christ living in me."*[26]

When this takes place, your will will no longer be running behind His, because His will will be yours.

Here then is the step we must take today: Always give what is "ours" to Him, more quickly, immediately.

This is the only way He'll take His portion and say to you: "Omnia mea, tua sunt." For you, the fullness of my joy. You can no longer have anything but me. Am I perhaps not enough for you?

And how would you answer Him, little heart called to Love?

For the Love of the Abandoned Love may you always more quickly give what is yours, to Love. This is the only way I'll be able to see Him in you.

Chiara

---

25. "All I have is yours" (Jn 17:10.
26. Gal 2:20.

L_{etter} 25

It's So Easy to Please the Lord God

Undated Letter from 1945
to Fosca Pellegrini

This is the first time in a letter that Chiara speaks about the Pact of unity and of consummated unity.

It is not certain what she is referring to when saying "Always read what I send you." She is possibly referring to her early commentaries on the Word of Life.

August 1945

My Dearest Fosca,

When I think of your last visit with us my heart is filled with gratitude to God. And I extend special thanks to you for having remembered me.

Now I believe that nothing or anyone will separate us.

My dearest Fosca, if you only knew how much I'd like to have you here with us for a while, so that our Ideal could be firmly established in your heart like a "tower that stands forever."

On the other hand, I entrust *everything* to Him for whom I do everything and live and rejoice and, in whose Name I've established with you a friendship that will never end.

Remember the Pact?

Consummated unity!

Onward!

I know: you'll fall. I also fall, often, always. But when I lift my gaze to Him and see Him there, incapable of revenge, since He is nailed to a cross because of His boundless love, I let myself be caressed by His Infinite Mercy and I know it's the only thing that must win out in me.

What good would it do Him to be infinitely Merciful? What good would it do Him, if it were not for our sins?

I would like you to be with me because the heart calls for nearness between souls who love each other.

But then I think that the One who built up the strength of Love within me is also near to you, very near, in the Holy Tabernacle!

You understand me, Fosca. I know. Well then, listen to me.

Go directly for the Prize!

If you have Faith (it's all here) you can understand me: Love? You want it? God is Love. And God is in the Holy tabernacle. There is where he waits for you! There is where he calls to *you*. There where he is exclusively "Love," he would like to pour out his inexorable riches upon souls who love Him and ... he doesn't find them.

Fosca, believe me:

God doesn't want many things from you except your heart.[27]

Give it to Him and you'll have given everything. It's so easy to please the Lord God!

Come on! Up! Don't object to any difficulty. Be children and God will be your Father, and will take you by the hand.

Tell your stories to the Living and Loving Jesus in the Tabernacle. He'll tell you about the value of life.

He'll console you.

... remember though that He, because of His great Love for you, asks for consolation *from you* and He wants for you to smile at Him over the tears, because, *loving you,* he suffers at seeing you suffer...

Always, always tell Him that your sufferings are nothing, that you don't even suffer, that life with Him is the most beautiful life. That you are the happiest daughter of the earth!

Only in this way, when you least expect it, He'll caress your soul and you'll feel that you are loved...

This is my wish for you, my Fosca.

Your Chiara

Do you want us to be consumed in the most perfect Unity? Always read what I send you from up here. Make it bread for your life — milk that nourishes my soul and yours and creates in us a single heart: the

---

27. Underlined three times.

Heart of the Adorable Christ. I always meditate only on these pages until they become my *life!*

Fosca, Fosca, if you love me, especially if you love Him, then do the same!

You'll see, you'll see!

Chiara

L*etter* 26

I'd Like His Cry to Become My Life

Letter of October 30, 1945
to "Eli" (perhaps Rosetta Zanoni)

Chiara had given the name "Eli"[28] to Rosetta Zanoni (see Letter 12). Nevertheless, the actual recipient of this letter is uncertain because in the first lines of the text her name is Elena, whose feast day is November 7. The theory that this is Rosetta, is correct if Rosetta took Elena as her Franciscan name from the Blessed Elena of Padua, a Poor Clare Nun who knew St. Francis and St. Anthony of Padua, and whose feast day is not the 7th but the 4th of November.

"The priest who gives us guidance" is Father Casimiro Bonetti, OFM CAP. *from Perarolo. We notice that Chiara calls the group of her first companions "the Unity."*

In this letter Chiara shares the essence of her life: the cry of the Abandoned Jesus, and it is interesting to note that what she calls "humility" here, she will later call "nothingness." The link between Jesus Forsaken and unity is mentioned: form for Him "a Paradise of Stars!"

---

28. "Eli" is the Italian rendering of *Eloi* as in *Eloi, Eloi, lama sabachthani* (Mt 27:46).

October 30, 1945

My Dearest Eli,

Your feast day is drawing near: Saint Elena — 7 November.

This is why I write to you, but also and, above all, to respond to your short message from which I drew true comfort and could feel that your heart was on fire.

Little Eli, you don't realize how much I love *you in particular.* And it's not for some human reason, but because something above human awareness unites us in the close bond of God's Love.

Think of how seldom we met. And yet I feel a growing fondness growing inside me, because I feel that you're with me, near to me in the ascent along the Way of Holiness.

And then you're my "Cry."

You know how beneath all things, in the deepest part of my soul, I carry my love for him Abandoned and how I would like His Cry to become my life in the most extreme humility. Because His Cry is the source of all humility: Jesus Forsaken, in extreme fulfillment of His Divine Mission, was constrained by the Divine Will to cry out the abandonment of that Father who was a single oneness with Him!

My Eli! Stay attached to Jesus Forsaken. Be! Be His living Cry!

Cry your name to the Eternal Father and to the Heart of the Blessed Virgin! Cry it for all of Humanity, for every sinner in the world, for all the Unity, for our girls, for the priest who guides us! Cry it from the depths of your heart: "But why, my God, have you abandoned me?"

Cry as if you were Jesus, for the Heavenly Father and the Mother of Jesus and our Mother cannot stand by and not come to our aid when they hear it! We are in such need of Heaven's help in forming on earth a Paradise of Stars for Jesus Forsaken!

Tell me in writing, my Eli, that you'll do what I'm asking. And I will feel the rhythm of your breathing as it continually rises to Heaven and I'll be able to rest assured as I await everything from Him.

Valeria will have told you that our teacher in the Way of God is Saint Clare of Assisi.

I want to give you a gift from her for the occasion. I send you a relic

---

29. "My God, my God, why have you forsaken me?" (Mt 27:46).

in the form of a thought written by Saint Clare in her letter to Saint Agnes of Bohemia. Take it for your own and make it the norm for your life, as I have done.

"But because *one thing is necessary* I bear witness to that one thing and encourage you for the love of Him to Whom you have offered yourself as *a holy and pleasing sacrifice,* that you always be mindful of your resolution like another Rachel always looking to your beginning. (A play on the word Rachel.) What you hold, may you always hold, what you do may you always do and never abandon, but with swift pace, light step, unswerving feet — so that even your steps stir up no dust — may you go forward securely, joyfully and swiftly, on the path of prudent happiness, not believing anything, not agreeing with anything that would dissuade you from this resolution, so that you may offer your vows to the Most High in the pursuit of that perfection to which the Spirit of the Lord has called you" (2nd Letter to Agnes vs. 10–14).

I pray that Saint Clare may bless you from Heaven where she is more luminous than ever.

Chiara

P*art* 3

"I have come to bring fire on
the earth, and how I wish it
were already kindled!"

(Luke 12:49).

L*etter* 27

Don't Let the Time Go By
Without Love

Letter of November 29 (probably 1945)
to Anna Melchiori

*Chiara had given Anna the name, Giovanna, "the disciple
whom Jesus loved," wishing to show God's predilection for her
and the beauty of following in the footsteps of the beloved disciple
who was near to Jesus all the way to the cross.*

*Jesus Forsaken is seen as the "giver of unity." Chiara invites
Giovanna to learn to discover Jesus present in every person and
to make every moment fruitful for Him.*

Ave Maria!

Dearest Giovanna,

Saint Clare! On this feast day of All Franciscan Saints, may she give to
you all of her Seraphic Flame and burning love *for our Abandoned Christ!*

Keep Him ever before you as the example of extreme love.

He is Everything. He is the giver of *unity.*

Giovanna, pray more (which means to pray well, very well).

Let Jesus pray when, *alive, he lives in your heart after Holy Communion.*

Let Him once again pray his final prayer to the Father that you may
be made worthy to work for the Greatest Ideal: *God.*

Always get up and walk again.

Remember that at the end of your life you'll be asked for the 7 + 7
works of Mercy. If you did them, you did *everything.*

And I'd like you to join us in living *the present moment and, in the present
moment,* the work of Mercy that God requires of us.

Do you study? = Do you instruct the ignorant?

Do you tutor a classmate? = You counsel the doubting.

Do you eat or give food to others? = You feed the hungry.

Do you drink or give someone a drink? = You quench the thirst of the thirsty.

Do you pray? Pray for the living and for the dead, etc?

The 14 Acts of Mercy could determine each of your actions.

And each of your actions can be turned toward Jesus who must live and grow in you and in your neighbor.

Thus you will go about doing good and irradiating Jesus all around you.

We know inasmuch as we *"do."*

Do, do, do!

"Coepit facere et postea docere."[30]

The same for you.

And you have so much to do! You have everything to do, if you don't love each other there as we do here.

Irradiate Christ by *loving!*

Don't let the time go by without any love.

Don't be forced to say: "I wasted the day!"

To the heights of heroism and of Love!

To the heights, to the heights!

Let your *deeds* cry it out: Unity or death!

Chiara

---

30. "Jesus began to do and then to teach" (see Acts 1:1).

59

L_{etter} 28

He is My Truth and My All

Letter from the early months of 1946
to Anna Melchiori

This is a particularly important letter because in it Chiara, who was usually very reticent when it came to her own story, confides autobiographical details to her friend Anna Melchiori. It seems to be addressed to all those who feel an attraction to the Truth and would like to become its disciples. The writer knows how easily this can remain at a low level of desire, for whoever wishes to possess Truth must become its servant, its "slave" and not fear "losing her own soul." Using the image of climbing a mountain, she appeals earnestly to her friend, whom she wishes to bring to the complete "vision of the unreachable immensity of God's Love," to free herself of the burden that's weighing her down. And, to help her in this, she reminds Anna of the name she once gave to her, "Giovanna" (see Letter 27).

Dearest Giovanna,

What you wrote made me so happy.

I feel the Lord working and making the chords of your soul sound with a very different melody than before. I willingly pause and write to share some of my thoughts with you.

Look, Giovanna,

I am a soul passing through this world. I have seen many beautiful and good things and I have always been attracted only by them. One day (one indescribable day) I saw a light. It appeared to me as more beautiful than the other beautiful things, and I followed it. I realized it was the Truth.

I desired to willingly become its slave because I immediately loved it and possessing it was my only true happiness. I passed some time unconsciously in this loving "service."

And, meanwhile, forgetful of the world, carried along by an instinctive need, I nourished myself each day on the Lord. Holy Communion was my preferred food, which I never neglected.

I then noticed (and some time had gone by) that my service to the Truth and my Love for that Food were identical expressions of the same desire.

It was *God* whom I saw and loved in that Food; and it was *God* whom I *loved* in the Truth.

Indeed, *Jesus* was the Ruler of my heart.

And I passionately offered my life to Him and I wanted, for love of him, to forget *all else* and to give up ... even my soul.

My dear Giovanna, why have I told you this story of mine?

Because *I feel that we are made of the same stuff.*

Like Chiara, Giovanna also wants to look Truth in the face and to commit follies for it, to rejoice in her own nothingness for it, and to turn her own world upside down for it.

My dear Giovanna! You're a child, you're intelligent, you're a student — but first you are a soul who God would like to kidnap and have for His own.

I feel Him working deep within your heart, and I always discover more and more proof that I'm not lying when I tell you that *you're made for the great heights.*

If you interrupt your ascent, you'll die in your desperation because your heart aspires to things that are lofty and pure and wide as the endless heavens.

See? I go through the world and touch many souls and all of them sing their song for me.

At times, most times, I hear a voice satisfied with the state in which they find themselves or for their aspirations that are a bit less petty.

But other times, rarely, I meet a heart which the Lord God has looked upon with fondness. Then it's a moment of glad rejoicing for me, because, with flying speed, I want to bring that soul to the full vision of God's immense and unsearchable Love.

You are one of these, Giovanna. Don't become proud: *"You did not choose me, but I chose you"* (Jn 15:16).

Tremble, rather, at the thought of inhibiting God's plan. So, like John the Beloved, abandon yourself to Jesus' Heart; rest your little head there where every ray of Light and all the Flame of Love is poured out upon the earth.

Giovanna, do you want to follow your Way? That *only Way* that you intuited deep in your heart?

Do you want to ascend?

The mountain bag is still full of humanity and the climb is hard. But if you wish, I'll help you.

It's a great joy for me to feel you close to me so often through your letters which show me what you're really thinking.

My desire to tell you what I'm thinking is like a sea that rises in my soul because of my Love for Him and Him alone, my Truth and my All — Giovanna, my dear Giovanna, will Jesus have in the 1900's, in this century of hatred, a new "Beloved Disciple" who loves Him above everyone else, no matter who that one may be? A new young John who, *full of strength and will and tender affection,* will stay close to Him at the foot of the Cross? Just when everyone abandons Him?

Will He?

Look at the wild ride taken by Saint Francis of Assisi.

Throw off that burden that weighs on you and prevents you from taking flight.

You should even lose your soul and never give it a second glance. Only those who straighten their gaze and keep it fixed on Him can be allowed to look at their souls, so that their own supposed goodness doesn't make them proud, and humility doesn't caress them with the delight of imagining themselves undarkened by sin as it is transformed into subtlest pride.

My dear Giovanna, raise your eagle eyes to His Divine Beauty which dies for you, for your blessed eternity.

Yes, feel the pain of having crucified Him with your sins.

And may *humility* (born of Love) and the *burning attraction* for Him in Whom you place all your confidence and hope, for Whom you fight and lose everything — be the pillars of your soul.

Always stay by my side.

Oh, that He triumphs in you, or death!

You know the immenseness of the Ideal that inspires us.

Don't look at the tininess of the one who professes it. Salvage It by *serving It,* and you'll have achieved your purpose.

Wishing you well,

Chiara

L*etter* **29**

Love Me, Chiara, Love Me!

Letter from October 3, (1946?)
to Sister Josefina and Sister Fidente

These two consecrated religious from Rovereto were probably Franciscans. Notice that this is the first written document which mentions the Testament of Jesus. Unable to find the words to communicate the fire burning in her soul, Chiara uses another means: She shifts to talking with Jesus, allowing the readers to listen in and be part of her prayer. Unity was by now a well-developed concept in Chiara's mind and this letter is a little treatise on living it.

Ave Maria!

"Grant me, O Lord,
that I may pass through this world
like a sea of Flames, setting everyone ablaze
with love for You!"

How happy I am, oh, my Jesus!

From your heart that is broken because of my many sins, from your heart, crazy with love for sinners and the most wretched: once again a Voice speaks and strikes me in the heart: "Love me! Love me, Chiara, love me! Despite your sins, despite your unfaithfulness and your wretchedness … Yes! Love me and make me be loved precisely because you were and are the most miserable creature on earth. You know the Heart of your Jesus and how he always chooses the most inane, useless, and miserable people to create the masterpieces of his mercy. You're the one I chose. I'll use you. Serve me with burning love. There are so many in this world who don't know me."

My Jesus, I believe that I am the most fitting instrument for what you mean to accomplish.

You and I know each other, Lord!

You know the infinite depths of my misery.

Like no one ever before, I know, love, and want to take advantage of the infinite richness of your Mercy![31]

Oh! Blessed and Open Heart! Blessed Wound! Allow me to expose you to the world, that a salutary shower of your Blood and your Grace may descend upon this earth and cleanse it of all its filth.

Oh, Saint Francis, on this vigil of love, unite our three small hearts in your burning heart. Make us into your Heart: the Heart of Jesus.

On this Vigil of your Seraphic Father's Feast day, oh Saint Clare, offer Him a gift. Gather into your heart which was victorious over all its enemies, illuminated by countless visions, enriched by the heroic Ideal of perfect holiness, these three souls who today become your daughters in such a special way. And promise your Seraphic Father that you will do everything in your power to cultivate them so that they can be your instruments, repeating in this world his anguished cry:

"Love is not loved!
Love is not loved!"[32]

Sister Josefina and Sister Fidente, my sisters!

I found a strong and singular desire in both your letters: to Love Him! Therefore, I decided to write a single letter to you both.

I know that each soul is a world unto itself and that the nearer it draws to God, the more it becomes a Heaven unto itself.

But, for the moment, I know only one thing about the two of you.

---

31. In Italian "misery" and "mercy" sound similar.
32. See footnote from the letter of December 1944 to her mother.

And I write to this *unity* of two souls already fused together in a single and burning desire.

What joy! In his immense goodness, Jesus grants that I find not only one heart, but two, for He knows that a *perfect Unity of two hearts cannot but be formed by Saints and that only two Saints can form a perfect Unity.*

Here is my advice:

1) To boldly reach your goal, you must aim at only one thing (which has a second part to it that comes as a consequence): *uniting yourselves to Jesus.*

2) Unite your hearts to each other with such *supernatural love* that it will overcome every divergence, every difficulty, and every obstacle that could arise between you. And extend this love to all your sisters.

1.

Union with Jesus.

My sisters, in speaking of this I would prefer to have you here beside me, for I'd like to watch and feel how deeply my words are penetrating into your souls. But if Jesus wants it this way, so be it.

He's the one that does everything.

To unite ourselves to Jesus (*which is our only goal in life, especially ours that have been given to the Lord*) there is only one means: *our sins.* We need to remove every other thought from our soul. And believe that Jesus is drawn to us solely by the *humble and confident and loving exposition* of our sins. Of ourselves we have and accomplish nothing but *misery.*

He, of Himself, has only one quality in our regard: *Mercy.*

Our soul can unite itself to Him only by offering Him as a gift, as our only gift, not our own virtues, but our own sins!

Because a soul that loves knows the preferences of her Beloved and knows that if Jesus *came on earth,* if He became *man,* if there is a deep longing in His Divine and Human Heart, it is only:

To be a Savior

To be a Physician!

He has no other desire. "I have come to bring fire on the earth, and how I wish it were already kindled!" (Lk 12:49).

It's a devouring Fire that *wants* to devour misery, to find misery and to consume it!

"Oh, Jesus, you know my incapacity! But you can work the miracle: draw these two hearts into the deepest understanding of your Mercy!

I know how the weight of your Mercy weighs upon your Heart, which is so unknown, because you have such an infinite Store of Mercy for men that *it could sanctify everyone,* and no one knows how to use it for your Glory!

Jesus, Jesus allow the hearts of these two Cyrenians to help you carry the weight of your Mercy and let them go through the world distributing it with open hands to every heart, so that everyone may be struck by your Immense Love and discover the way that leads to You Our Complete Happiness!"

My sisters, go to Jesus often, *always.* Confess your sins to Jesus *in every moment,* to Jesus living in your hearts.

Gather each imperfection, each imperfect sentiment, each fruit of your humanity which you are bringing along behind you.

And offer it all to Him!

With humility, which means being conscious and certain that you have nothing else to give to Him that is truly *your own.*

With love, which means with gusto and all projected toward the Beloved; certain that He looks at you with much more love, the more you confess to Him the *subtle intricacies* of your malice, and you will be dealing your self-love a more precise blow.

With confidence, which means with the certainty that he desires nothing more than "to be the Savior," nothing more than to exploit His Blood, nothing more than to sanctify you! What good would His mercy do Him, in fact, if He weren't able to find misery? Jesus — Mercy desires nothing but misery![33]

We believe.

It's Faith in His Mercy that we need to enkindle within us. And we should implement this Faith in *each moment.*

Concluding this first part:

Let us be united to God in this way:

    a. *with confidence* (I believe–know–am–certain, and I act according to my faith in His Mercy);

---

33. Chiara is playing with the sound of two Italian words: *miseria* (misery or wretchedness) and *misericordia* (mercy or compassion).

b. *through our miseries* (gathered in each moment and offered with humility and confidence and love).

Oh then! How much Heavenly Grace: How Jesus opens the Wound in His Holy Side allowing the miracle to shower down! He'll work in us and change all our misery into a Flame of Love for Him. *So it is.*

2.

Be one among yourselves.

May each of you no longer see Sister Josefina or Sister Fidente in each other, but only Jesus! Tell Jesus that the proof and the measure of the Love that you bring to Him is the love that you have between you for Him!

Love means that the total will is projected toward God giving our heart to Him in each moment, our mind, all our soul. And, *for Him*, giving all our will, all our mind, all our heart, and all our soul to the sister (the measure of our love for God) for whom we desire the same holiness as we desire for ourselves.

Love each other. And you will have done everything.

By loving each other you'll learn how to love all the sisters in the same way.

My sisters! I must leave you now.

Yes, yes, Jesus must grant me this grace.

"Jesus, open the hearts of these two little Brides and inscribe upon them your Testament, which you spoke as you turned toward your Father on the night before you died:

'Holy Father ... (may) they be one *as we are one*' (see Jn 17:21).

Then seal their hearts so that they may become depositories of your ultimate words, the wonderful summary of your Gospel, the perfect synthesis of Love.

And make them go through the world crying out everywhere through the holiness of their lives that no Ideal is more beautiful than that of fulfilling here on this miserable earth the ultimate desire of a God who dies of love for us."

And may She *in whom is found the grace for every Way and every Truth*, be your teacher! Our Lady is very happy to see us all focused on fulfilling the desire of Her Son!

And you, my sisters, whom I dealt with double confidence, for I already see you there in Heaven, close to my own soul: sisters of a single Father, of a single Bridegroom, of a single God, following the Lamb wherever He may go — listen to my plea:

From within your silence pray for one only grace for this poor soul, that grace which makes me pleasing to God:

The most absolute poverty of spirit = in the deepest humility.

With immense affection,

Your little Sister Chiara
Viva Jesus!

L*etter* 30

If You Don't Pray, Why Are You Alive?

Letter of October 14, 1946
to Sister Josefina and Sister Fidente

Chiara disputes the praise she probably received from these two religious sisters and vigorously corrects them with love. She returns again to speaking directly to Jesus. She wants for her companions what she has for herself: God alone. For the first time she mentions "a vast field of action that reaches to the ends of the earth." The episode of the feast day of Christ the King probably occurred on the last Sunday of October 1945.

Hail Mary, Mother of God!
October 14, 1946

My little sisters,

Since I love you in Jesus, allow me the full liberty of the Truth:

Maledictus homo qui confidit in homine!

"Cursed are those who trust in mere mortals!" (Jer 17:5). Your little sister, Chiara, might have so much love for you that it couldn't be contained by the whole world; she could, as you say, be inspired by the Holy Spirit; she could reach the highest level of Holiness; she could promise her everlasting faithfulness to the friendship that's begun between us... But Chiara still remains a miserable daughter, an imperfect human who is a paralytic when it comes to doing good, and ruins the work of God.

How foolish is the one who trusts in another!

My little sisters, I know what you're saying. But *since I love you,* allow me to move you from your half-way state and cast you to the Heights, into the very heart of the Most High.

"Blessed are those who trust in the Lord!" (Jer 17:7).

"God of my soul, my Love, my All, You speak to these two little hearts. Speak with Your Divine Voice.

Tell them that *You alone are Everything* and that You live in them!

Tell them not to search for you outside of themselves, but to always find you there, in their heart!

You know already, Jesus, how much I love them and always want to be with them. I, your Bride, would like to be with You in every heart that is in grace, to make You be loved! But I can't. I am and still remain a human being.

You are God! You, Spirit Most Pure who penetrates everybody and dwells at every moment in the hearts that love You!

Oh! Beautiful Jesus! How far from You even those souls that are Consecrated to You and should give everything to you — their thoughts and affection — to You living in them!

You say it to them: Why don't You triumph in the world?

Why aren't you loved?

Why aren't you known?

Because everyone is searching for You where you will not be found.

Because those who *should trust in you completely,* refuse to seek You! *Oh! How truly greedy the person for whom God is not enough!*

Speak to your Brides.

Tell them that Chiara could die one day. They could lose any direct help from her; that human beings, precisely because they are human, are destined to pass away. That any person who trusts in another person merits a curse from You!

God alone is Everything!

And this Truth must be lived out through a burning love for Poverty!

When is it that we love You, Lord?

When is that we've found You?

When is it that we can be sure of having found You?

When we *trust only in You and madly turn our gaze on high and seek* only You:

God–Our-Father!

And now that your Brides are stripped of everything and are convinced *that You alone suffice:* now speak to their hearts telling them that you also accept (as I also gratefully and joyfully accept) the burning love that I bear them and the heartfelt desire to make of them what my heart would like to be for You!

Only the Saint who has left everything and has the gaze confidently fixed in God can return to the world and gather the sweet fruits of holy friendship that God the provident Father has destined for them!

My little sisters,

How can I bring you a few slivers of gold when I know that in your heart you carry an inexhaustible gold mine?

There, in the center of your heart, Sister Josefina, is where God lives!

There, in the center of your heart, Sister Fidente, is where God lives!

Place your hand over your heart.

You are tabernacles of the living God.

Live in this Faith and it will be impossible for you not to become saints.

Voice of Light { 1. Listen to His soft Voice
2. Talk to Him when He doesn't speak.

This is the life of the saint: an ongoing conversation of love. ("There is need of only one thing" [Lk 10:42]!)

My little sisters,

How much good your life could accomplish, similar as it is to the life of Jesus when He lived and worked and loved in the little house of Nazareth!

But don't you realize that a soul who lives in this way, living *life as a couple* (Jesus and the soul), does as much as if she were out preaching to the entire universe?

Now that you are stripped of your misery, which you will daily give over to God, you are free to love

Love!

He wants to live with you. And there's nothing He desires more than this *life as a couple*.

It's only by being closely united in your individual souls with Jesus, that you'll strengthen *the unity between the two of you* more and more!

"Father ... that they may be one as we are one — I in them and you in me — so that they may be brought to complete unity" (see Jn 17:23).

"Jesus, may Sister Fidente and Sister Josefina be one, as you, Jesus, and your Father are one.

Your Father in You. You in the heart of these two small Brides, so that they may be consumed in that unity which is You, Yourself!"

I conclude, my little Sisters, by entrusting myself to your prayers.

You know that my field of action is vast, reaching to the ends of the earth!

There's so much to do in the world!

"The harvest is plentiful" (Lk 10:2)!

Pray, pray, pray that God's love will take root in the heart of every person!

Pray, because if *you* don't pray, why are you alive?

I love you so very, very much,

Chiara.

Viva God!

Letter 31

We Must Be

That White Host of Virgins

Letter of December 8, 1946
to a group of youths who were close to her

This letter is addressed to young women who did not live in Trent but still belonged to the "white host" of those consecrated in virginity. There were forty of them. With Chiara they had begun a journey toward affirming this choice. She had written their names on the back of a picture of Our Lady to seal their pact. This was a practice of hers that was dear to her throughout her life.

To the Immaculate Queen of Virgins

My Sisters dearest among all,

You who are far but joined to me in a particular way by the one and the same Ideal of Unity and Virginity, I send you greetings today from the white host of virgins who, for the first time have secretly gathered to begin the cultivation of our souls for virginity![34]

We all placed ourselves (all 40 of us) in the Immaculate Heart of Mary and we wrote our names (I wrote the names of you that are far but so present here among us) on the back of the picture of Our Lady that adorns our living room wall.

It's been already three years since I was alone in consecrating my life to God by the hands of the Immaculate Virgin.

Now there are 40 of us!

---

34. The word "host" means a huge "array" or "crowd" of virgins. The color white is associated with virginity, the "white martyrdom" as opposed to the "red martyrdom" of blood.

A white host of souls who, like ivory towers, must support the entire Ideal!

Virginity or death!

We face a nearly invincible fortress that must be overcome: the world, the devil, sin! "Only lilies can overtake a fortress."

Gathered together for a few hours on this sunny morning that's been made even brighter by the Immaculate Virgin, we placed ourselves under the protection of Saint Agnes, Virgin and Martyr; and of Saint Ambrose, the saint of virginity.

We wish to imitate Agnes in the total gift of our young lives, in the powerful force of our purity that cries out in its immaculate splendor: "Unus est dilectus meus!" ("Only one is my love!")[35]

If a saint has said that only a host of virgins in every city can save the world, then *let us be that host!*

We read such marvelous things about virginity, written by Saint Ambrose.[36] May your guardian angels convey to you some of that divine atmosphere which filled our hearts and, just as in those times when mothers locked indoors their daughters who had fallen in love with virginity and wanted to run after the Saint and hear him speak, so too for all of us, drawn by the sweet voice of the Mother, of the Immaculate Virgin, let us swear faithfulness to the Spouse of virgins for the coming of God's Reign in the world.

We all send greetings.

Set your gaze High beyond stars and Angels in the very Heart of God from whence Virginity descended to the earth, that eminent virtue that reaches beyond nature and makes us into angels.

Be like angels passing on their way to Heaven, like angels, so that you can be angels in Heaven.

In the Immaculate Heart of Mary,

Sister Chiara

---

35. Free translation of the *Song of Songs* (perhaps 6:3).
36. See Ambrose, *De Virginitate.*

73

*L*etter **32**

Be Dauntless and Active
in Doing God's Will

Letter from Christmas 1946
to the young people who followed her

This letter witnesses to the fact that unity was the only focus of Chiara's life, but it is also a testimony to her teaching method. She leaves but a single word in the souls of her listeners, a "Yes" that echoes throughout the Scriptures and is expressed in many different ways. "For the Son of God, Jesus Christ ...was not 'Yes' and 'No,' but in him it is always 'Yes'" (2 Cor 1:19).

Christmas 1946
Unity or death!

Dear little sisters near and far!

Our deepest and most heartfelt best wishes!

We've never felt as united as we do this Christmas.

Yes, let's swear to it: Unity or death!

And our gift is also for you who do not yet know the "nice things" that the Lord has recently given us, so that all of us together, enriched by the same Light, may meet at the foot of the manger equally loaded with Gifts.

Listen carefully:

We know each other: we've been overwhelmed by a most luminous Flame: the seraphic Flame, the Flame that consumes everything (extreme poverty), the Flame that illuminates and warms everyone (infinite Love).

Let yourselves be burned: be poor even of all the beautiful things you have learned up till now.

Re-clothe yourselves in our Flame which, this Christmas, has taken on such unique and forceful warmth.

Yes!

Yes! Yes! Yes! A determined, powerful, complete and active "Yes" to the will of God! Let us go the manger overflowing with gifts.

All of us, with impassioned hearts let us say Yes! Always! to the will of God.

Why are we still so imperfect? Why still so many sins? Why are we not yet fused in a single unity which would be able to offer the splendid flower of perfect joy and the delicious fruits of: Heavenly works!

It's because we still do our own wills!

If we all do God's will, we'll very quickly become that Perfect unity that Jesus wills to be here on earth as it is in Heaven!

Little sisters near and far who are drawn by only one splendid idea, let us gather at Christmas midnight before the Holy Child and cry out with hearts deep in prayer:

Yes!

I assure you, if we say it with all our heart, with all our mind, with all our strength: *Jesus will live again in us* and all of us will be another Jesus, going about on the earth and "doing good."

And isn't this our Dream?

And if this yes is repeated with equal intensity at every moment of our life, then we'll really see coming true what we've asked for so much and wished for so much as our Christmas gift:

Being Jesus.

This is what I ask you all to do. Because God has placed a magnificent star over us, His particular will for each one of us. By following it we'll all be united in Heaven and we'll see many other stars following in our Light.

Again, I ask and implore all of this for you.

Chiara

L_{etter} 33

Only One Idea: Unity

Letter of January 1, 1947
to the young women who followed her

Chiara now addresses the topic to which the Spirit has led her: unity. This letter reiterates and summarizes the previous themes of "God alone" and the will of God. Love leads us to the point of being "consumed in one."

New Year 1947

Dearest sisters near and far,

I've received so many letters in the past few days that I don't know how I'm going to answer all of them. Little by little, I'll do my best, for I love all of you, each and every one, as I love Jesus who in His infinite goodness has given you to me as sisters in this Faith[37] that must conquer the world.

Your letters clearly tell how much He desires that we be united and how our heart speaks only one word which gives peace and consolation to us: God.

May we all remain united in Him. May we stay firm in our great intentions.

Our Faith that He loves us will provide us with the greatest conquests.

Do everything I tell you, so that you don't fall into the folly of one who knows what to do and doesn't do it.

Keep one idea fixed in your head.

It was always a single idea that made the great Saints.

And our idea is this:

UNITY.

---

37. Faith in God's immense love.

"Yes, Father!" We're Jesus! Likenesses of Jesus in every moment responding again and again to His will: Yes, Father! "Yes, Father!" Yes, yes, yes, *always and only yes.*

This *yes* will make you share in our unity that exists only in God.

His Will binds us and consumes us in Him and among ourselves. Yes.

Unity: I want it. I want what He wants,

His Will or death.

Unity: direct ongoing communication with God through radical mortification in the present moment of everything that is not God. I want only God. He alone is Everything!

Unity: between us, in this stupendous community of souls scattered through the world, enclosed and sealed only by the love of God!

My sisters, the world has its allurements and those who are content to be in it.

Don't be of the world. Be opposed to the world. Despise the world. It leaves only bitterness and melancholy in your soul because you have been made for Heaven. Remain in the world to suffuse it with the scent of lilies, and, with your life, shout it out in a loud voice that your trust lies in the One who has conquered the world.

Unity with your sisters will provide you with strength and courage and help, because we believe in the communion of Saints.

You know the world is cold and we, who want to give everything to the only One who has truly loved us in time and in eternity, should always keep our soul aflame.

And when the coldness of the world threatens, let us raise our gaze on high to where so many souls have gone before us. Let us call on the Saints and consume them in unity with us so that we will remain faithful till death and receive the crown of Life there above where we all expect to be together forever, seeing, contemplating and loving Jesus, the only bond that has joined us from near and afar.

Chiara

Letter 34

Jesus Crucified,
the Greatest Book of All

Letter of January 5, 1947
to Sister Josefina and Sister Fidente from Rovereto

*Making reference to the superiors and to the small commu-
nity, this letter could be addressed to two sisters. This is the first
remaining document in which Chiara refers to the new commandment of Jesus as the "pearl of the Gospel."*

*This letter brings out the exclusive and fervent love that for
three years Chiara has been nourishing toward Jesus Crucified
and Forsaken. But it also shows the link that runs between his
cry of abandonment and the unity he asked of the Father in his
final prayer, his testament (see Jn 17:21).*

Vigil of the Epiphany
The Holy Name of Jesus

Dearest little sisters,

So many times I wanted to sit down and answer your letters personally, but I just didn't have the time.

You understand, my little sisters.

Finally, after so many days, I send you at least a thought, the thought
that summarizes our entire spiritual life:

Jesus Crucified!

There's *everything* — the best book of all. He is the synthesis of all
knowledge. He is the most ardent Love. He is the perfect Model. He
is the Ideal of our life.

Let's have Him *as the one and only Ideal* in life.

It was He who led Saint Paul to such holiness.

It was He who made Saint Francis into the Saint closest to the Heart of God!

Dear little sisters, may you always, in each and every moment, have Him before your hearts, which are so burning and desiring to love.

May your love not be sentimentality.

May it not be reduced to a mere show of compassion and the shedding of a few tears.

Let it be *conformity*.

Keep Him before you as the *Ideal*.

Then plunge yourselves into the Divine Will.

The more it makes you similar to Him, the more you'll grow in joy, *because you'll always be achieving the Ideal more and more.* In the accomplishment of the Will of God, which lies entirely in *loving of God and neighbor to the point of being consumed in Unity*, you'll find the Cross on which you are to be crucified.

Don't be frightened! Rather, be glad! Reach for your Goal!

Jesus needs souls who are capable of loving in this way:

They *choose Him*.

Not because of the joy that comes from following Him; not because of the paradise He prepares for them nor for some eternal reward.

And not just to feel all right.

No, no, no. Jesus needs souls who, only because they are thirsty for true love, want to be one with Him, to *consume their souls with His*, with that Divine Soul that is so sorrowfully torn to death, and constrained to cry out: "My God! My God! Why have you forsaken me?" Oh! My little sisters, we have only one *life and it's short at that*. Then Paradise! Then forever with Him: We will follow the Lamb wherever he goes!

Don't let *the suffering* frighten you!

On the contrary!

Suffering or death!

But seek the suffering that is offered to you by the *Will of God*, not only what is commanded by the Superiors in the simple commands of obedience, but that which is the Will of God: *mutual Love — the New Commandment — the Pearl of the Gospel!*

Do everything, *everything you can* to be *one* with each other and with all your sisters. They are your neighbors, so *love them as yourselves.*

Today is the Feast of the Holy Name of Jesus and, *in the name of Jesus, I ask the Eternal Father for the grace that He will hasten the hour when all of you will be one, of Only One Heart, of Only One Will, of only one thought:*

Which?

Jesus Crucified!

Then, drawn by the Cross which draws all things to itself, you'll be working to form *your little Community into a single block* and — in this — you'll give *Greater Glory* to God!

But to achieve this, it's necessary that you empty yourselves to *Jesus Crucified*.

Those who've sworn to the Ideal live of Him!

Don't complain then, if the Ideal costs you something. You belong *to the Ideal. And you sing with the only happiness that can be called "perfect."*

In conclusion, I will ask you a question, so that you may have the full measure of my joy.[38]

Do you think that Jesus could contradict himself?

No, never.

Well, Jesus says: *"My yoke is sweet and light."*[39] And so it shall *always* be. Forward, then, with courage! Even if it means being crucified like Him:

Live the present moment and, in that present moment, love as He loves, so that as you come closer and closer to the Ideal you'll feel that each yoke is easy, each burden sweet!

Chiara

---

38. See Jn 17:13.
39. See Mt 11:29.

Part 4

"Whoever is near me
is near the fire." [40]

40. This is an ancient apocryphal phrase attributed to Jesus. Pope Benedict XVI cited it in his homily on the Solemnity of Pentecost 2010. Chiara uses it in Letter 25.

81

Letter 35

Unity is Jesus

Letter of August 6, 1947 (from Assisi)
to Father Raffaele Massimei, OFM CONV.

At the end of January 1947, having come across some bro-
chures which spoke about unity, Chiara went to meet the priest
who was distributing them in Rome, Leone Veuthey, OFM CONV.

Aside from distributing these brochures that gave comfort
to Chiara, Father Veuthey began a "charity crusade" in which
Chiara and those who followed her willingly participated. He
would later refer to them as apostles from Trent where "300
persons were prepared to take up the crusade" (D.M. Pieracci,
Scritti di Paola Morani, 1988, p. 110).

Through her relationship with Father Veuthey, she came to
know many of the Conventual Friars Minor including the recip-
ient of this letter, Father Raffaele Massimei, OFM CONV.

Father Valeriano Valeriani, mentioned at the end of the let-
ter, was delegated by Father Veuthey to organize the crusade in
Assisi.

This is the first document in which we find written the expres-
sion, "Jesus among us" and it is the first time that Chiara invokes
Mary as "Mother of Unity."

The Transfiguration 1947

Reverend Father,

I'm responding to your telegram right away.

Father Casimiro wrote yesterday, informing me that it will be
impossible for him to go to Rome or to Assisi where he was invited to
the Spiritual Exercises being given by Father Valeriano. His superiors
didn't allow it.

"Do *whatever* he tells you" is the Word of Life for this month and …

Father Casimiro by *not coming* and … you by *not coming* in order to conform yourself to the Will of God, show that you are perfect Crusaders. Isn't that so, Father?

There were so many times when I wanted to write you and to your Crusaders. But, since the Lord didn't want it, I believe that He took it upon himself to speak to you in your hearts.

I feel you near, Father, one with us in the Heart of Jesus!

Oh! Unity, Unity! What divine beauty!! Human words are not able to express it!

It's: Jesus!

I would like to overflow and pour into hearts all the Light that God, in His mercy, gives to me.

This morning at the tomb of our Father, Saint Francis, I prayed for you, as I do each morning, but today I especially asked all the Light of Unity for you. It will come.

Pray for me, Father, or better still, *pray that all may be one*! This is what it's all about.

I work with perfect joy.

I'm *certain* that God could not have chosen anyone but me for this task, because … I know Him and I know what He says:

"Your nothingness draws me, your weakness fascinates me. *I would change your dust into a magnet that will draw souls.*"[41] Father, it is with miseries that you move forward! How unclever of Christians not to take advantage of that little bit of sludge that they have in their hearts! Mercy … would be left unemployed if it were not for souls who keep it working with their weaknesses!

I always pay for the light and the love that God gives me with my miseries.

And for this reason I always have enough for others too.

Father, you be clever too! Even now, the only thing we have in our souls that is truly "ours" is the evil that we've done, right?

* * *

Maybe I'll see you in September. I'm happy, very happy, because I feel you closer than all the other priests!

How good the Lord is.

---

41. Perhaps this is a sentence from Saint Bridget of Sweden, cited by St. Alphonsus Maria de Liguori in his book, *The Glories of Mary*, part one, chapter 6, § 3.

Perhaps the Lord has ordained for you to make a special unity with the Crusader Priests!

I'll pray to the Eternal Father in the name of Jesus at the tomb of the Seraphic Father...

It will happen!

Let's be one — always:

Trento ＞ Jesus ＜ Rome

that Jesus be among us!

Greet every, every, every one of your souls. Tell them that I have a special love for them as I love Jesus.

Give a blessing to your daughter,

Chiara.

I'll be in Assisi until the 13th. I have many opportunities to pray with our two Saints. Anything for unity.

"Mater unitatis ora pro *us*!"

Mary Wants Us United

Letter of September 6, 1947
to Carmelina and friends

Carmelina was a young woman from Anagni, an ancient city southeast of Rome, who together with friends had come into contact with the Movement. They were waiting for Chiara to come to Lazio in west central Italy. Here for the first time Chiara cites the sentence from the Gospel of Matthew, "For where two or three are gathered in my name, there am I in the midst of them"

(Mt 18:20), which is so important in the experience of Chiara and of the Focolare Movement.

Here Chiara begins to place the Word of Life in the heading of her letters.

We see Mary taking on a major role in Chiara's life, and she herself will state the reason for this when she responds to a question put to her by someone who asked why she spoke so little of Mary: "[...] Those who live unity are the ones who really and truly love Mary. [...] Mary is the doorway which brings us to Jesus. The doorway is not a doorway if it isn't open, allowing us to pass through. The Blessed Virgin is this nothingness, this emptiness, this oblivion, this self-forgetfulness, this purity... This doorway is for Jesus. [...] Those who live unity possess Jesus and are therefore the ones who really and truly love and appreciate Mary."

Fiera di Primiero, September 6, 1947
"Do whatever he tells you!" (Jn 2:5)

Dearest Carmelina and friends,

In a few days we will get to know each other personally.

But already we are *one* in the Heart of Jesus and in the *Immaculate Heart of Mary*, right? I'm so happy to be writing you on this first Saturday of the month!

It's the Blessed Mother who desired for us to meet on the Path of God's Love.

All of us were already walking down this shining path.

Our Lady wants us to be *united on the way!* She knows that "where two or three" unite in the holy name of Her Son, *"He is among them!"* (see Mt 18:20).

And where Jesus is, danger flees and obstacles vanish. He conquers everything because He is Love!

Therefore, let today be the day of our encounter, the day of our unity.

It is Mary, who, taking us by the hand, melds us in unity, more and more, to the point of consuming us in it!

Forgive me for writing in pencil, I'm in the mountains.

Sister Chiara

I greet you each and every one, together with all the souls who share our struggles and our Ideal.

L_{etter} 37

The Light is Where There is Jesus

Letter of September 6, 1947
to Irene Maragliani and friends
from Anzio (Rome)

This letter is addressed to some people Chiara had met during a previous visit. In this letter she underscores the link that exists between unity and Mary (see introduction to Letter 36).

"Do whatever he tells you" (Jn 2:5)
Fiera di Primiero, September 6, 1947

Dearest Irene and friends,

It's been such a long time that we haven't seen one another!

And yet, the more time goes on, the more we're united.

Don't you feel it?

How is it going? I know, my little sisters. You have been sorely tested by so many things and that is why I'm even happier as I join near to you again, because I feel that *Jesus loves you more.*

Today's the first Saturday of the month. It's such a total joy for my soul to be able to reunite with you in the Immaculate Heart of Mary!

I'm convinced that She is the one who wants Unity! Mary, Mother of Unity.

The Blessed Mother wants us to be saved, and she wants the greatest number of souls to be saved.

She knows Satan, his flattery, his tricks, his traps. And so she calls her children to unite and walk in the Way of Love.

Because where two or more will unite in the name of Her Son, *Jesus will be in the midst of them!*

And where Jesus is:

there is Light Love strength,

omnipotent strength that draws everyone into the Heart of God. *Arrivederci* Assisi!

Sister Chiara

Forgive me for writing in pencil, I'm in the mountains.

L*etter* 38

Burst Through the Dams

A letter of November 6, 1947
to a group that includes both the young and the old

Chiara had met these people during a short "run through the area of Rome" in some neighborhoods she doesn't mention.

In this letter Chiara develops the idea of "Jesus in the neighbor."

November 6, 1947
"Those who abide in me
and I in them bear much fruit" (Jn 15:5)

Dearest little sisters,

After my return from Lazio, I am with you again, remembering each and every one of you whom I love as myself: both young and old!

My run through the areas around Rome left in my soul a great desire to love Him and to make Him be loved!

How many, how many souls are awaiting our Ideal to give wings to their heavy lives, their boring lives, their overly useless and lonely lives!

And how many beautiful souls which, in contact with such a great flame, would flower and be abundantly fruitful. Whereas, isolated and on their own are barely, barely, able to stay good among so many who ... "forgive them; for they do not know what they are doing" (Lk 23:34).

How, how many, if only they had met someone with a Big Heart, a heart as wide as His, would never have fallen, never have known the evil that perhaps has now left its indelible mark on them!

My little sisters, stand up and be ready to cast your life into the greatest Ideal of all! Burst through every dam. Deny yourselves so that you can gather into your tiny–great hearts all the sufferings of the world! A neighbor passes beside us in each moment! It's Jesus. Measure your love for God by the love that you bring to that neighbor.

Remain "in him," in his sufferings, in his needs, in his fears, his concerns, in his doubts, in his occasional joys. "If you remain in me ... you will bear much fruit."

Oh, then, how the Flame of divine charity will grow to be gigantic! How Jesus will grow in you and devour all of you! Allow him to grow, and you die. Allow the Charity which He has spread in your hearts to inflame, to blaze, and to come out sparkling from your eyes, from your words, from your actions.

Let God reign in your hearts!

Let him act!

Don't oppose yourselves to His action.

"Whoever remains in me and I *in Him,* will be the one to bear much fruit!"[42]

Yes: *Jesus* in us. Love that unites hearts and that makes us all of the same idea: *His,* all of the same will: *His!*

Jesus in us will bear much fruit.

All your sisters from up here send you greetings, they are *one* with you and they wish you everything that God desires from you.

In the Immaculate Heart of Mary,

Chiara

---

42. "Him" is capitalized, referring to Jesus.

L_{etter} 39

Unity's Secret

Letter of March 13, 1948
to Father Bonaventure da Malé, OFM CAP.

This letter is addressed to a Capuchin father who had heard about these young tertiaries when he was still a student at the college run by his order in Trent, and had met Chiara.

Taking her cue from her own painful experience of making herself one with other brothers and sisters, she speaks to him of Jesus Forsaken as the One who gives us the strength for overcoming all the difficulties in unity. Jesus Forsaken is "unity's secret" and he is the "founder" of the Ideal (the Ideal "came out" from him). Chiara breaks into prayer, in a hymn to Jesus Forsaken, the way of holiness and salvation.

> *"Stay awake and pray*
> *that you may not come*
> *into the time of trial"*
> *(Mt 26:41)*
>
> *March 13, 1948*

My dearest brother in Jesus,

I so much enjoy feeling you so close, in fact, one with me and with everyone in the Unity. You know that Unity is Truth. And for the sake of the Truth, which is Jesus, I will tell you this. Some time ago, a long time ago, I suffered greatly as it seemed to me that you were not so united to my soul; once I had felt you united.

Every time I don't find myself perfectly melded in unity with a soul, I experience this "spiritual laceration;" truly as if part of me has been torn away.

During my last trip to Rome I had to change my mind, because I found you very close. Unity is such complete joy! And what a bitter cup is even the slightest disunity!

And disunity lies there wherever love is not perfect, imperfect when dealing directly or indirectly with souls.

I've found many such "lacerations" and perhaps (certainly) it's because spiritual– self– love has thrived and continues to do so.

Our soul's cry which is Jesus' cry: "Unity or death!" is the strength and the reality of each day.

Honestly, Brother, if I didn't have before my eyes the most painful cry of our beloved Jesus: "My God, my God why have you abandoned me?" my life certainly would have been buried by the endless difficulties that I encounter in consuming myself with souls. Every soul is Jesus who breaks out in that most painful cry.

He almost no longer felt the force of the divinity within him then, for it had gone hidden into the depths of his soul and he felt such infinite inconsolable grief.

My Jesus! Reduced almost to a mere man, in order to make us God!

How close Jesus feels to us in that human cry!

Such strength in such terrible pain!

I'd like to be near you my brother, not only with letters as you want, but moment by moment, to speak to you of Him reduced to such sorrow!

That's "*my* Jesus!"

I've never spoken to you like this. But I've revealed the secret to unity for you.

That's where we've found it. He gave it to us in that cry, when, in the sum of his misfortunes that plagued his humanity, he wanted to experience disunity with His Father, precisely as he sacrificed himself for the Father, being nailed to a cross. Mystery of suffering so deep; deep as God.

God abandoned by God! He is Man because of (his) infinite love toward man, to whom he has given God. Jesus was never only man, but he experienced this infinite laceration from the Father in order to experience what "mortal sin" signifies.

Jesus! The Holy! The Pure! Love Himself!

He gave us Unity: the ideal which is God himself; Holy Spirit, who joins the Father to the Son and whom Jesus abandoned no longer felt

90

for a time on the Cross so that we would never feel ourselves abandoned by God! From that heart which was spiritually crushed and destroyed with suffering infinitely greater than the physical wound, the Ideal came out.

I adore that spiritual suffering, brother, because in it I find Light, Love, and Life. It was and is everything for me. It's the precious hidden pearl for all those who want to purchase Unity.

With Him you pass over every obstacle, because He is the greatest suffering, and in Him we found rest and an infinite resource for each tiny laceration to unity.

But like Him after crying out the abandonment and abandoning himself to the Father and dying in Him — so too for us: looking to our model, we are able to recompose Unity wherever and with whomever may have broken it.

Jesus Forsaken, all for us! How I thank You and adore You for having opened my heart this evening, to be able to say to this brother who, already loving You, perhaps had not yet focused his soul's loving gaze on Your greatest suffering!

You illuminate him on how to penetrate that endless treasure trove of light and love which You are in your abandonment! You are the peak of self-giving! You are the life of the Trinity on the earth.

God who gives God to God! You're the God of unity.

You're the life for every death!

You're the resurrection of the dead to the life of Your grace!

You're the forger of saints!

You're the passion of the souls that are thirsting for unity!

You forever console in the nights of disunity and you provide us with the strength to recognize even and the most difficult disunity!

You are everything!

I adore You! I love You!

Let the world find the way of salvation and holiness each day in You!

Happy Easter to you, Brother, and to all the souls that are united through you to Jesus!

Resurrect! Love!

Pray for me.

In Jesus,
Sister Chiara

Letter 40

The Bride Must Resemble the Bridegroom

Letter of March 30, 1948
to Father Bonaventura, OFM CAP.

In witness to the strength and light that Jesus Forsaken provides for her to compose and recompose unity, Chiara continually finds new ways to present this topic, this mystery of love and pain, understood and yet never understood, infinite as God. When she speaks of Jesus "reduced almost to a man," she means it in the same way as in letter 38 "reduced almost to a mere man."

This is the first document in which Chiara signs her name, "Chiara of Jesus Forsaken," her "surname" as she will later call it.

> *"My God, my God, why have you also abandoned me?"*
>
> *March 30, 1948*

Dearest brother in Jesus,

When I received your letter, I headed for the city ... only Jesus could see the joy that overcame my entire soul.

Yes, it couldn't have been otherwise.

I'm convinced that unity in its most spiritual, most intimate, and profound aspect, can only be understood by the soul for whom God has chosen, as her only portion in life ... Jesus forsaken who cries: "My God, my God, why have you also abandoned me?"

Brother, now that I find an understanding of this in you, of this which is the secret of unity, I would like to — and I could — speak to you about it for days on end. Know that Jesus forsaken is everything. He's the guarantee of unity.

Every light on Unity stems from that cry.

Choose him as the only scope, the only goal, the only arrival point for your life and … generate an infinity of souls to Unity.

The book of Light that the Lord is writing in my soul has two sides: one, a page shining with mysterious love: *Unity.* The other page, shining with mysterious pain: Jesus forsaken. They are two sides of the same coin. I show the page of Unity to everyone. For me and for those who are with me on the front lines of Unity: *Our only portion is Jesus forsaken.*

We've chosen to climb the mountain toward extreme abandonment.

Unity is for the others; for us, it's the abandonment. Which? The one that Jesus (reduced nearly to a mere man in order to deify us) suffered: extreme pain, the sum total of all suffering, the pain as great as … God! "My God, my God why have You also abandoned me?" And we search for him like the spouse in the Song of Songs — This is our supreme duty as those who have been thrown into the front lines by infinite love.

Search for him in our brother sinners … without God! There He is crying: "My God, my God…" Search for him in the external abandonments, but especially those that are deep and hidden … All the ones He sows along the path of life.

Brother, there's no fuller, no more bitter joy than when the soul is suspended between heaven and earth — alone with Him alone, who is abandoned even by the Father and still God!

Ah, brother! If you throw yourself on this path, you will very soon experience the stigmata of the Abandonment! Then the Lord will carve an infinite emptiness in your heart … which you will immediately fill with Jesus Forsaken.

And you'll never be alone. On the contrary, you'll enter deeply into this mystery of love and of Pain, and you'll understand it all, and you'll never understand it. But you'll love it, and love will give you the strength to unite what is "detached."

Brother, not everyone understands these words. Let's not give them to just anyone. Let the Abandoned Love see himself surrounded only by hearts that do understand them because they have felt him passing in their lives and have found in him the solution to everything.

For the others, Unity! For us, the abandonment! Yes, because the bride cannot be dissimilar to the bridegroom.

Jesus is missing God. In order to console Him, let's promise Him to offer Him always the presence of Jesus among us. "Wherever two or more ... there am I."

Jesus will console Jesus who cries. My Jesus! Our Jesus!

Chiara of Jesus Forsaken

*L*etter 41

Serve Jesus in Everyone

Letter of April 1948 to young women
who had entered the communities
called the "hearths" or were preparing to enter

The date of this letter was recovered from a work of Igino Giordani, according to whom the letter was written to bring about cooperation between Catholic forces, with the first free elections in the Italian Parliament, following the War, April 18, 1948. Chiara signs the letter with three asterisks as she was in the habit of doing at that time. The letter is addressed to "the hearths" which had not yet separated from the Franciscan Third Order or from the Crusade. The focolarine without work in the city were: Aletta Salizzoni, Ada Schweitzer, Palmira Frizzera, and Giosi Guella.[43]

This letter offers some simple and profound rules of wisdom regarding how to comport themselves with the people around them, then Chiara leaves it to God to illuminate each one of them.

---

43. The Italian name for hearth is "focolare." Consecrated men or women who live in these small communities are called "focolarini" (men) or "focolarine" (women). Chiara writes to the focolarine who belong to the women's "focolare" in Trent.

Dearest *focolarine*,

When the Lord who "reproves the ones he loves" (Prv 3:11–12), puts me to bed, I have more time for seeing things clearly concerning you and concerning me.[44]

What I say to you today I would like you to take as *the precise will of the Lord* and the beginning of a new kind of life that should fascinate you just as the motto of yesterday and always fascinated you: "All or nothing!"

"You are the *light* of the world and the *salt* of the earth" (see Mt 5:13–14), but the light of the world *should illuminate* and the salt, *salt*. Otherwise, what are they good for?

Well, ever since the beginning of the new year we've been saying that the Franciscan Third Order (and much more, the *Crusade*) don't have personal initiatives, but only the single task of evangelizing themselves through love, and then to belong to everyone, at the service of all, servants of all.

This is our Ideal! You will be able to tell the value of our Ideal *by the works that we do:* That they may see our good works and glorify our Father in Heaven.[45] But do them only *for the Lord God!* Not just to do them — not to be seen — not for you — But for Him! This alone will have to suffice if you are truly to be most ardent workers: *flaming Fires.*

Here are my counsels:

Occupy yourselves with these during *all of the time* that remains from *your duties* of work and study and the life of the hearth (this goes for the extern *focolarine* as well).

Present yourselves to others *serious and united*, but not in an irritating way; give yourselves to the hardest tasks — without measuring.

If you don't have time, find it: A saint finds time for everything. For your holiness, this formula is sufficient:

Work like a hard laborer

and pray like an angel.

If you obey me in this, I assure you that you won't fall into the heresy of activism.

---

44. Chiara was evidently confined to bed because of illness.
45. See Mt 5:16.

1) *Have a big heart, loving everyone.*
2) *Always have a smile on your face.*
3) *Keep hard at it*: This is the only way to become saints. If in the evening you don't go to bed tired, then your day has been spent in vain. Promise to do only *what is really possible.*
4) For those living in the hearths, who are without work in the city (Ala, Ada, Palmira and Giosi), the advice is: offer two hours a day to those tasks that are of direct service to others.
5) Find someone who *follows* you and is living outside the hearth, but very faithful and very trustworthy. (Send me the names.)[46]
6) I assure you that God will bless our Work in proportion to our disinterest in ourselves and the love that we have for others.
7) Let no task be repugnant to you. Look at Jesus and Saint Francis the beggar, and recall that holiness means winning out over our selves.
8) Without letting them feel it, stay under the authority of Graziella and of Giosi. They have equal power between them: Graziella depends on Giosi and Giosi depends on me.
9) All that I've told you is absolutely necessary for *really* loving God.
10) Above all, in all that you do, let the following always reign among you:

A completely supernatural spirit that makes us see Jesus in everyone, appreciate everyone, judge no one, make comments about no one (It's time wasted), make yourselves the last in order to be the first in the kingdom of heaven, serve Jesus in everyone,

Bring Unity into every environment.

The Lord God illuminate you.

* * *

---

46. It is uncertain what Chiara means with the phrase "follows you." It could mean someone like a priest to accompany the focolarine in their spiritual lives, or it could refer to someone from outside the house to look after them in their dealings with the local environment.

L_{etter} 42

Let Everything Else Crumble — Unity Never!

Letter of April 1, 1948
to Father Valeriano Valeriani, OFM CONV.
and to his confreres in Assisi

Father Valeriano Valariani was the right-hand man of Father Veuthey for the Charity Crusade (Letter 34). The post scriptum is addressed to him.

The "external unity" mentioned here was a group of persons who lived for unity without yet becoming permanently involved. The Father Luigi, whom she asks to be greeted, is Father Luigi Marvulli, OFM CONV.

Chiara once again takes up the topics that have begun to stand out in her soul: unity and Jesus Forsaken, finding still newer ways of linking these two mysteries, while always returning to her first intuition of: God and God alone. There is no dichotomy between God among us and God in us; the one guarantees the other.

"Stay awake and pray that you may not come into the time of trial"
(Mt 26:41)

Trent, 1 April 1948

Dearest brothers in Jesus and sworn to Unity,

I'm finally able to write you.

But I assure you that my soul, our souls, were always one with yours.

We prayed for you *as* for ourselves. And just as we desire for ourselves to bring greater Glory to God through the unity of our souls in love and in truth, so too do we desire this for you.

We have only one Father: the one who is in Heaven. Only one Mother: the Virgin, Mother of Love. Only one brother: blessed Jesus by Whom we are all brothers with the same spirit!

Brothers, Let everything else crumble — unity never!

Where there is Unity, there is Jesus!

Put your three young hearts together and form a single Heart: the Heart of Jesus!

Be the real hearth of Assisi.

Always have this Fire burning among you.

And don't be afraid of dying. You've already experienced that Unity requires the death of everyone, to give life to the *One!*

Over your death, *Life lives!*

The *Life* which, unbeknown to you, enlivens so many souls.

Jesus said so: "And for their sakes I sanctify myself, so that they also may be sanctified in truth" (Jn. 17:19)

To accomplish the Unity of all Assisi and the world, stay *united with each other.*

It's the only way.

That *Unity* in which Love dwells will give you strength to face every external disunity and to fill every void.

Do this as your sacrosanct *duty*, even though it brings you immense joy!

Jesus promised *the fullness of joy* to those who live Unity!

And don't be afraid of anything. Fear only that you might attach yourselves to something that is not *Jesus among you.* This is your and our Ideal. *Jesus among you* (who brings you *among us*) is also the guarantee of *Jesus within you* in the most complete unity with Him! In fact: We've loved Him all we can when we are dead for Him (who lives *in our brother*).

Enjoy your *unity*, but for God and not for yourselves. Saint Catherine of Siena admonishes us to love God for God, our neighbor for God, oneself for God, never for ourselves. Our unity too, which is our sanctity, should be *loved for God*! Let's make the *Unity between us* (which gives us the fullness of joy, peace, and *strength*) the springboard to run and jump to wherever there is not unity, and *make it happen there!*

In fact, just as Jesus preferred the Cross for Himself and not Mount Tabor, let's also prefer to be with those who are not *in unity*, so as to suffer with Him and to ensure that our love is pure love! Then let us bring these conquests that the Lord has given us into the little sheep-fold of Jesus: Unity.

And it's for this reason, Brothers, that we crusaders of Unity have chosen as our only Goal in life, as our Everything:

Jesus Crucified who cries: "My God, my God, why have you also abandoned me?"

This is Jesus in maximum Pain! Infinite disunity so that He can give perfect Unity to us, which we will be able to reach only relatively here below and then completely in Paradise.

This Jesus who is suffering so infinitely is in need of consolation from us. And what is lacking to Jesus in such anguish? What medicine that would heal his pain?

God!

He's missing *God!*

How can we give God to him?

By staying united we'll have him among us and Jesus who is born from our unity will console our Crucified Love!

This is why we should increase our Unity in its quantity of love and of souls! We want the King to be magnified among us! And so we'll go out seeking to recompose every disunity, and even more, because in every disunited soul we hear the cry of our Jesus groaning more or less strongly.

Brothers, let us love Jesus especially by being the angels of His Abandonment!

I've experienced that every soul that finds itself on the front lines of Unity can only hold out by drawing on a Suffering–Love as strong as that of Jesus Crucified!

Now I leave you! Countless souls are waiting for a word, assistance, comfort. Let's run to them! Let's lift them all up.

Let's love everyone.

Among us, the pact is sealed!

May God make you burn with Love![47]

Sister Chiara

Father Valeriano,

I don't know if those who have sworn to unity with you will agree.

You, who were among us, be the interpreter for them.

---

47. A saying of Saint Catherine of Siena.

Greet the external Unity of Assisi for me and all the others I know, especially Father Luigi.

Unity marches on.

We can do all things because He is *among us*.

Sister Chiara

$\mathcal{L}_{etter}$ 43

If Only the World Knew Him

Letter of April 23, 1948
to Father Raffaele Massimei, OFM CONV.

Before settling in Rome in 1949, Chiara took several trips to the capital of Italy. In this letter she speaks with total openness about her impressions of their meeting to Father Massimei who already knew the Ideal of Unity.

"Humility, self-emptying, is the virtue that unites the soul to God. Even the tiniest amount of human nature that doesn't allow itself to be assumed by the divine life, breaks unity with serious consequences."

"Stay awake and pray that you may not come into the time of trial."
(Mt 26:41)

Trent, April 23, 1948

Father Massimei,

There was "something" between us, Father, "something" imperceptible perhaps, but it was there.

This "something" that I noticed the last time you came to Rome was and is perhaps "something that's missing," an impossibility I feel regarding you that makes it impossible for me to be able to communicate all the Light to you, not even the tiniest bit of it.

What was the cause?

Certainly it was a deficiency of love in me and, perhaps, also in you ... because it is enough that one soul be what she should be so that others will find themselves being what they should be.

May I speak clearly?

May I cut this subtle chain that often makes me depart from you with an inner and indescribable anguish, certain that what was in me wasn't able to flow into you and our unity be complete?

Father, I always talk news with you, I never give my soul to you with the Light of God.

I talk like this because I don't find that perfect emptiness in you ... and the Light of Unity, which is — so my Superiors have informed me — Light of God that can only dwell where there is the most perfect emptiness. You need to lose everything in order to find it again in God's Fullness!

Losing everything means *"everything,"* without holding anything back, without judging. Then, when we're this "crazy," we have the Wisdom of God!

I see — in your letter and in some of your expressions — that you don't have the spirit of unity because you make distinctions: groups of souls and ... your office as Father Provincial.

No! There is only one thing you must do: Be one with God and when you are, you are one with everyone. One with God who wants us to do his will moment by moment. Perhaps your way of expressing yourself is an expression (of God's will), but already this expression doesn't give you perfect peace, the peace that a soul has who is in the will of God.

At times the will of God is pain, abandonment, and torture. Allowing the will of God to be *the only "preference" of your soul* means rendering without fail the unity of our soul with God and therefore with our neighbor.

The Unity up here (in Trent) is now moving forward in this light:

Seeking (which means finding and possessing) *God in His will, in the present moment* (as it concerns us) and always embracing It.

Among all the painful moments, prefer especially the abandonments

101

of the soul, because this is where our crucified and abandoned Jesus who "espouses" the soul is found.

This preference, which at first is always an act of the will, soon becomes heartfelt, and then you throw yourself into a sea of pain and you find yourself swimming in an ocean of love, of perfect joy.

Like so...

We've observed that every pain of the soul (not of the body) can be annihilated and the soul can feel itself filled with Holy Spirit who is Joy, Peace, Serenity.

This holds for those who follow in our path without fear or doubt.

It's so strange, Father, the more I find souls — almost always souls of consecrated religious who think about these things ... and who don't understand — the more I have light about this possibility of conquering the death (which is *non-love*) of the soul (without — Light, without — Joy, without — Peace) with the Life which is:

Christ Crucified and Abandoned!

He's Everything!

If the world only knew Him!

If the souls that follow Unity only sought and welcomed Him as their only goal, as their All! Then Unity would never again suffer imbalances and breakdowns.

Try, Father, to embrace Him.

If I hadn't had Him in the trials of life, there wouldn't be Unity, unless Jesus brought it about somewhere else.

Jesus Forsaken won every battle within me, even the most terrible battles.

But you need to be crazy with love for Him, the sum of all pain of body and *of the soul:* medicine, therefore, for every pain of the soul.

You need to seek only Him, crave only Him; and when He draws near to your soul, rush out and embrace Him and find your Life in Him!

Your health is down today, with new rheumatic pains in the back that sap the strength from your entire body and constrain you to bed. This is Jesus Crucified too. Hurrah!

Until next time.

Give me your blessing,

Chiara.

Greetings to everyone!

Letter 44

He Accomplishes the Impossible

Letter of April 29, 1948
to a group of consecrated religious

This letter concerns some Conventual Friars Minor from Assisi. The "F. G." to whom Chiara refers is Friar Girolomo D'Alonzo, belonging to the same order. The signature "S.C." stands for "Sister Chiara."

This letter's simple clarity leads its readers into the unspeakable light of God, and opens before them a vast mission, vast as the entire world.

April 29, 1948
Ave Maria!

That all be one! (Jn 17:21)

Dearest brothers in Jesus,

I can also say to you what F.G. said to us: All of us know you because I have known you and made one of you known to our sisters and, in him, I think all of you are present.

Unity!

But who would dare speak of it?

It's as ineffable as God!

You feel it, you enjoy it ... but it's ineffable!

Everyone enjoys its presence.

It's peace, gladness, love, ardor, an atmosphere of heroism, of highest generosity.

It's Jesus among us!

Jesus among us! It's living to have Him always with us! It's creating Him — understand my meaning — among us in every moment. It's bringing Him into the world that is oblivious to His peace. It's having His Light in us!

His Light!

I want to talk to you and I don't know how.

The voice of the heart is love.

The mind contemplates, filled with the beauty!

I wish the whole world could crumble, but that He would remain among us, among us united in his Name because we are dead to our own names!

Brothers, the Lord God has given us an Ideal that will be the salvation of the world! Let's remain faithful to it, whatever the cost, even if one day we have to cry out with our soul in flames because of the infinite pain: "My God, my God, why have You also abandoned me?"

Onward! Not with our own shabby strength, but with the omnipotence of Unity. I've seen, touched it with my own hands, that God among us accomplishes the impossible, the miraculous! If we remain faithful to our charge (that all be one) the world will see Unity and with it the fullness of God's Reign. All will be one if we are One!

And don't be afraid to surrender everything to Unity: without loving — without measure — without losing our own judgment, without losing our own will, our own desires — we'll never be One!

Wise is the one who dies in order to allow God to live in him!

And Unity is the training ring for these fighters for the true life against a false life. Be consumed by Unity. Never leave each other until everyone feels that he is included. Unity before all! In all! After all! Discussions count for little, even the holiest of questions, if we don't give life to Jesus among us by loving each other so much as to give each other *everything*.

I'd like to tell you so many things, but ... what would it serve? I know that I'm writing to brothers in Unity, and that it's already like Paradise among you by now: each one seeing himself in the other and taking delight!

The Lord bless us all and use us for his Design of Love.

S.C.

L*etter* **45**

Jesus Forsaken is All For Us

Letter of May 10, 1948
to Father Raffaele Massimei, OFM CONV.

This unsigned letter, undoubtedly written by Chiara, lays out frankly the requirements of the "new way" brought by the Ideal of unity.

The term "kill" is attributed to Saint Francis, who used it figuratively to express the spiritual battle against the passions, what Saint Paul calls "the old self" (see Eph 4:22).

The "Unity of Rome" stands for the group of people who lived "the Ideal" of unity there.

"Set your hearts on things above"
(Col 3:1)

Trent, May 10, 1948

Reverend Father,

Since I can, I'll answer your letter immediately.

Father, perhaps my words will irritate you because — knowing how to remove from myself any half-measures (and this is because of the superabundant Light that the Lord has given to me) in order to reach my goal, that is, the fullness of life in your soul — I will play all the parts: the daughter, the sister, and the mother.

Then you decide, Father, whether to believe and accept it or not. And I'm sorry. "Love moved me which compelleth me to speak."[48]

I believe that you should not impose any other task on yourself other than that of sanctifying yourself. And you will do this by *sanctifying others,* the Jesus next to you in each moment, in your neighbor, communicating to him the light that you have received from your life

---

48. Dante, *Inferno,* Canto II.

experiences in living according to the Ideal. You'll have the fullness of life if you communicate it to others fully, in accordance with their ability to receive it.

"Always give your *all*" — that relative "all" — to others.

If you do this, you'll always be filled with life. If you economize, you'll be empty. And don't worry about all the other souls. If you care for the "Jesus" whom you serve in the neighbor who is at your side, Jesus will take care of your soul.

Otherwise, He won't. This has been confirmed a thousand times by experience. Then the *Blessed Mother* will take care of forming and finishing Jesus in you ... and without all the effort. It's enough that you recognize her as your *Mother* — that's all.

Of course I'll pray for you, Father, especially, and soon you'll be seeing the fruits. *You've suffered much.* Thanks be to God! From now on, desire only those moments. The Spouse of your soul — forever Spouse of Blood — is closer to you then and can enjoy a bit of relief at seeing his brother, his friend, carry the Cross for Him.

But realize, Father, that it is absolutely not our vocation to suffer pains of the soul. They'll be still be there, but we have to overcome them, and we can — always — as long as Jesus Forsaken is everything for us. My Jesus Forsaken, my All!

Be glad to suffer with Him and continue to love him by doing his will. Suffering passes. Our vocation is Unity — the fullness of joy.

If we don't have it, the fault is ours.

Up here, Father, things are always better. Miracles of Unity!

From everywhere in northern Italy souls are being called (many consecrated religious and priests) who want to be united to us. Unity is omnipotent.

Doing it matters. Don't let it end in chatter or in questions of propriety! But in facts. Dead to ourselves, so that Christ may reign.

Also the Unity of Rome (from the echoes I receive up here) is in need of *leaven* to raise the mass. But good leaven, fine leaven: *Jesus.*

That is, *few* souls who are *ready for everything,* fused together and *determined* to consume everyone else in One. Cultivate these separately in a very small group. You see how.

Otherwise you'll be limping. After killing himself, Saint Francis killed others. Loving others can sometimes mean inconveniencing them. You can do everything if you ask everything from yourself and from others. We need to love others as ourselves and to push them as we push ourselves. Let's hope for everything for each other. It will be given…

Bless me.

Letter 46

Unity in the Beginning, in the Middle and in the End

Letter of May 11, 1948
to Father Bonaventura, OFM CAP.

The light that "has choked me up with its overwhelming heat as it tries to escape," is so strong that the author can express the absolute, the ineffable only in short, epigrammatic phrases. In this letter she summarizes the entire way of unity with these few words: "It's God: Unity-Trinity."

An interesting element is the Marian aspect of the spirituality that comes to full blossom.

As the last part of the letter reveals, the recipient was in Fribourg, Switzerland. This is why he was less informed about the spreading of the spirit of unity.

The small "booklet on Unity" to which Chiara refers is the one that Father Leone Veuthey was distributing (see introduction to Letter 35).

Brother in Jesus and in the Seraphic Father,

I don't know what I'll write to you either. The Light, all that Light which God has given to me (thanks to an extreme triumph of his mercy!) chokes me up with its overpowering heat as it longs to escape. Vehemently...

Your letter confirmed the thought that I had about your soul, *so loved by the Lord* and, in a moment, in a flash, I'd like to give you all of mine, all that God has constructed within me, upon my nothingness, my weakness, my misery. We would have to die in our pain since we are not able to do it at once, were it not for our awareness that God (the Author of all) can do all things.

I believe this.

You believe it.

You'll see the results of this faith in you.

I tell you one thing: The Ideal we've embraced is *God: Unity–Trinity* and so it's as ineffable as infinite and eternal Love. And because of this, it's immanent, *present* (as God), even in the tiniest things, even in the smallest events!

God, Love, guides and does all things.

Even from the evil we commit (the only thing that is truly ours), he is able to draw greater good than the good that the evil had taken away.

And so it was He who desired that our two souls meet. There was a reason for our meeting, and what a luminous reason. When two souls encounter each other in the name of Christ, Christ is born between them; that is, *in them*. And by remaining in this unity, they can truthfully say: "I no longer live, but Christ lives in me" (Gal 2:20).

The important thing is to put *unity* at the beginning, the middle and the end. In this unity willed by God the two souls are melted into *one*, and they resurface *equal and distinct*. Just as in the most holy Trinity.

Jesus wants this in his Testament, which is the summary of everything he thought!

The thoughts of God!

"May all of them may be one, Father, just as you are in me and I am in you" (Jn 17:21). What I mean to write to you today is that we must never break this unity that's been established by God.

And in my soul, which I bring to you in this letter, there are thousands of souls who think as I do and are fused with my own soul. And in the soul that you've brought to us, we've welcomed all those whom you love and live for, all whom you would like to merge in *one* in fulfillment of your love for the Lord God.

Maintaining yourself in unity, you'll begin to feel the *strength of Jesus* instead of your own strength; the *Light of Jesus* instead of yours; the *love, the mercy of Jesus* for every one of your neighbors, instead of your own.

And Jesus in you will be: "Love, that denial takes from none beloved..."[49] that is, that *infinite* love that *always* wins out.

"*Omnia* vincit Amor,"[50] and the souls will be indissolubly linked to you, and they will bring you to God. Just so!

Because this is how God wants it.

He wants you to be Jesus, another Jesus. Our Mother in Heaven, Mother of Light and of the Divine Love, Mother of Unity, will bring about this miracle in you if you recognize Her for what she is: She is the "*indispensable one*" in the sanctity of whomever.

And she's the deposit of every grace. She's the one who generates, nourishes, and cultivates us as she did the "First Jesus." Even if we don't recognize her, she silently does it all. Why, she would do *everything that she did for her first Son* if only we would be dependent on her as a newborn is dependent on its mother.

Brother, we believe that it isn't necessary to communicate everything to be apostles of unity.

Let's do as much as we can to be united to the Unity (especially spiritually) and Jesus will be our "wireless telephone." After all, to be one, nothing more is needed than that both of us listen to his subtle voice, which *always* speaks in us. In the present moment let us live Christ who is speaking within us.

You've asked me for some detailed news about the movement. It would take volumes. When God works, what wonders come forth from His hands.

Saint Catherine said it: "If you are what you should be, you'll put fire in all of Italy (the world!)."[51] Don't be happy with small things,

---

49. Dante, *Inferno, canto V.*
50. "Love conquers all," Virgil, *Bucoliche, 10,69.*
51. See Letter 10. (See Letter 163 to Friar Bathelemi Dominici and to Friar Tomas d'Antonio.)

because He, the Lord God, wants great things! Let's believe this in unity. We'll obtain it, and God will obtain it through us, working through us.

And we want all the peoples of the earth for our inheritance. He said it Himself: *Postula a me et dabo tibi...*[52] Let's believe Him in unity.

We'll obtain it, and God will obtain it through us, working through us.

Let's allow Him to operate. May we never impede his omnipotence with the meanness of "our" views. We don't have a book or anything in print that states what we want. Our *only* book is the Gospel as the Church interprets it. In particular, it's the prayer addressed by Jesus to the Father.

Someone wrote something that came out in a small book called "Unity," which I'll send to you. What's written there is in accordance with our idea, but it doesn't say (in a complete sense) what we want. Actually, not even we know what we want. Only Jesus knows. And He knows that we have no other desire than to actualize his Testament as the best expression of our love for Him. He'll do it through us. We're always executing the details of this wonderful design. From the Beyond we'll see what we've accomplished. And it shall be the beginning of a Unity that will have to tie in everyone with the sweet bond of Love.

We begin the work here below. We'll continue it there above through the souls that will follow us.

Father, if you'd do me a favor, ask me anything you want: I'll answer. Then you'll make it easier for me. Otherwise (the Ideal is so vast) I won't know what to touch upon that would interest you.

And we have believed in Love! Saint Francis isn't going to be happy until you relive him and make him be relived in his brothers. Just begin. You'll succeed. *"Go, let it be done just as you believed"* (Mt 8:13). *And we have believed in Love.*

Goodbye and huge wishes of Unity from all the brothers and sisters.

In agreement we ask for your blessing and for all of Switzerland to be put on fire by you!

May God set you on fire with Love!

S. C.

---

52. "Ask me, and I will make the nations your inheritance, the ends of the earth your possession" (Psalm 2:8). See introduction to Letter 24.

We've Found the Precious Pearl

Letter of June 15, 1948
to Father Massimei, OFM CONV.

With a few light brushstrokes, Chiara reveals her personal situation and that of the Movement: sufferings, difficulty, approvals, disapprovals, even the possibility that the Movement might be disbanded "after six years of building." This letter reveals an inalterable faith in God who comes to meet her in Jesus forsaken, who is "complete joy" and "Jesus" and "Love."
Father Leone is Father Leone Veuthy, OFM CONV.

Trent, June 15, 1948
... seek the things that are Above...
(See Col 3:1)

Father Massimei,
    Thank you for your postcard and constant remembrance.
    I feel it.
    In these days of acute suffering and mad joy, I've seen, felt, and experienced with the soul that *Unity* is not the Hearths, the Crusade, the distance, approvals, or disapprovals. Unity is Something beyond all these things. It's Heavenly Peace — it's complete joy — it's perfect Light that illuminates the thickest darkness — it's pure and ardent Love ... it's:

Jesus.

    And He's sufficient for us.
    We watch — and perhaps we'll continue to watch everything fall apart. This would be the logical consequence of what has occurred over these days. "Logical" according to the finite vision of men, but not according to God who can — with an amazing miracle — salvage everything and make all things new.

And from amid all this destruction — after six years of building — nothing will be taken away from us. Love is intact, stronger, more beautiful and singular in the center of our heart, in the center of our Kingdom of souls! Those who felt fearful before now draw near to us because they feel *safe*. The timid ones are now waiting to see the results in order to then say that it was thanks to them that we have won!

How many — especially the ones in the hearths — feel stronger now, stuck on the Rock which is *Jesus* — ready even to die for Him.

And *Unity,* this impalpable, untouchable, invisible Something *rises up and dominates!* It's totally spiritual — all Spirit. But it's *Real, Concrete — it satisfies the soul and makes it sing.*

Oh! Father, what a Way the Lord has given us! How wondrous! Such a gift!

If only you knew what is happening among us and within us.

Satan's repeated attempts to make everything fall apart are proof of how much this Work matters to God.

But Satan can't get away with it.

God is invincible!

They give us Unity, we have God!

They take away Unity, we have Christ on a cross who cries: "My God, my God, why have you abandoned me?"

And he's God! Even though He cries. Precisely because he cries: The beautiful God of Love who gives the world a gift as big as God!

And He is our passion! Deep and sincere passion.

The other day I was saying — perhaps to Father Leone — that Jesus Forsaken is truly "ours" because no one wants Him: neither Heaven nor earth! Refuse of the world and of Heaven. Nothingness. *God.*

Oh! We've found it Father, yes, we've found the precious pearl! [53]

Oh! Our Love!

Oh! That piece of a Man, that "worm of the earth,"[54] He's all "ours!"

Oh! How our soul, which has discovered Him, lets go of everything in order to embrace only Him. Like the Bride in the Song of Songs, she sets out in search of her treasure! She loves Him and *adores Him!*[55]

What lover wouldn't be drawn by such a Love?

---

53. See Mt 13:45.
54. See Ps 21:7.
55. See Song 3.

112

Father, I'd like to run through the world, gathering hearts for Him. And I feel that all the hearts in the world would never be enough for a love as great as God!

Father, give me yours. Together with mine we'll form *Jesus* and Jesus is *God* and *God* will satisfy — at least a little bit — that infinite longing, that infinite pain!

Jesus, my Jesus, so mad with Love for me! How I see you! How I love You!

Lavish the heart of this soul that I feel so near! Consume it in you! Give it the momentum of infinite love! Rob it of everything so that it can possess only you and find, in your crushed Heart, the Way of Heaven, the most perfect Sanctity.

The Blessed Mother desires it.

Chiara

Love and Suffering are Synonymous

Letter of July 1948
to all members of the nascent Movement

The painful situation described in the previous letter is confirmed. Chiara speaks in strong terms of "persecutions," but always from within the context of a faith that is alive. And she mentions the very near dawn of resurrection.

Chiara draws very important lessons from her experience of suffering love, and she would like all those who are with her to be at the same level as she.

According to the devotional practice of the time, July was the month of the Precious Blood. Chiara notes that the Word of Life had just arrived from Assisi, which had been approved by Bishop Giuseppe Placido Nicolini from Trent and had been made the Abbot of the Benedictine Abbey of Cava dei Tirreni.

"H. H." stands for "His Highness" which was the title given to bishops from Trent, who historically were princes.

Chiara signs the letter "Charity-Unity," the name given to a pamphlet included in a diocesan newspaper, "L'amico serafico," which bore the imprimatur of the Trent diocese. The first edition of the newspaper came out in April 1948. The name "Charity-Unity" was meant to indicate what Chiara defines in this pamphlet as "a unifying movement that (...) would like to realize the unity of the world in Jesus" and "not a new association alongside the many that already exist."

The priest to whom Chiara writes in the postscript is probably Father Massimei, OFM CONV.

> *"et sine sanguinis effusione, non fit remissio" (Heb 9:22)*

Brothers and Sisters in Unity,

It's the month of July, month of the Precious Blood, the ultimate and most powerful expression of infinite love.

The Word that should illuminate the present moment of our life is:

"... And without the shedding of blood, there is no forgiveness" (Heb 9:22).

For any work to be of value in God's eyes, to have "divine" character, to work conversions and the sanctification of souls — it must be bathed in blood. Also "Unity," this movement of souls dedicated to the fulfillment of Jesus' ultimate desire, had to offer its blood for the sake of it.

Anna Magnani, our sister in the Ideal, was so dear, so on fire for her and our Ideal. A few days ago she was the victim of a tragic accident. Before dying she murmured the name of the priest who assists the movement up here in Trent, of some of us, then ... she said *she was offering the ultimate sacrifice, that of her life, for the Unity, because she knew it was in the midst of a full persecution.*

Now Anna is looking down on us from Heaven.

Her blood cries out to the world and to the devil who is furiously opposed to this work, which is the cry that arose from Jesus' very Blood: "That all be one!"

The tiny victim of that Divine Will, which she had learned to adore among us, now urges and ensures us. The Lord is with us. Unity will not fall.

We too, Brothers and Sisters, who have our eyes still open on this world, we too can offer to the Lord a coin that has value for the realization of that Ideal that no suffering will be able to rip from our heart.

Accomplishing the Divine Will perfectly, moment by moment, brings a struggle with it, which is comprised of *renunciation, sacrifice, death of the self.*

Moment by moment, let's gather these little drops of blood and offer them to the Eternal Father in union with the Blood of Jesus and of Anna.

Love and suffering are synonymous in the earthly life.

Perhaps, before, we found comfort, ease, a false peace, calm, and taking life lightly, in a way that was pleasing to us.

Now the only things that should fascinate us are those that are related to pain, struggle, zeal, a life of death to ourselves and life to the Divine Will. "…and without the shedding of blood" (Heb 9:22).

And so how can we be frightened by the persecutions, murmurings, misinterpretations, being called crazy, fools, fanatics, or of being abandoned by all?

Or might not these exterior and interior struggles be the very things to strengthen us more, to purify us before God, to make us worthy to be more similar to the Master in being hated by all?

When we're faithful to the Church in whatever it may command, when we don't break unity for any reason whatsoever because unity is God's sacred desire, when we put all our confidence in our Heavenly Mother and have her as the Queen and Mistress over all that concerns us, then we go forward singing the eight beatitudes, ready to shake the dust off our feet and to ask God to clarify everything in the next life and, in this life, ask only for His overabundant blessing upon those who, without wanting it, do us wrong.

May *Jesus among us* united in his Name command, guide, and provide the victory to his little army in battle.

And let us cry it out again with our life of love for God and for each other that the God Man has given us but one command in which all others converge:

"Love one another. Just as I have loved you, you also should love one another. By this everyone will know that you are my disciples, if you have love for one another" (Jn 13:34–35).

Charity–Love

Reverend Father,

It's the Word we took for the time being, as we awaited the arrival of the one from Assisi, which only came on the 7th of July.

We'll print that one next month.

Things are moving ahead well. "The 'happy day' is drawing near," said H.H., who is convinced that everything was happening for the good of the work:

1) so that it would be known;
2) because it became more known;
3) because they have documents (the accusations) on file, that will more clearly show what the work is all about.

Therefore … Thanks be to God! And thanks to all those who took it all in by taking upon themselves all the pain and all the joy.

Give us your blessing.

Sr. Chiara

(P.S. I'll write soon.)

$\mathcal{L}_{etter}$ 49

Nothing Matters Outside of Holiness

Letter of July 16, 1948
to someone she doesn't know

Chiara informs this person of what she said to the "Mary"
Unity (referring to the focalarine who formed the core group of
the Movement), that is, that the "trial" she refers to in the previ-
ous letter has passed.

There is not a word of bias against anyone who caused the
trial but only recognition of their helpfulness in providing "the
seal of God" and high esteem for their holiness.

Father Beda was most probably Father Beda Herneggar,
founder of a Regnum Christi Movement in 1950.[56]

The Father Provincial of the Conventuals from Umbria was
Father Vittorio Costantini, who later became General Minister
of the Order and then Bishop of Sessa Aurunca in Italy.

To the "Mary" Unity

Saturday, July 16, 1948

Dearest,

I'm sending you a brief report of what I said today to the "Mary"
Unity. I'm happy to tell you, for your joy and ours, that the trial we
went through, which you surely heard about, has passed. And it all
turned out for the best. If you only knew! How well the Lord does
things! Now the recovery will be even more beautiful than things

---

56. This Regnum Christi group, founded in 1950 by Franciscan Father Beda Herneggar, is not in any way connected with the Regnum Christi Movement founded by Father
Maciel in 1959. During the pontificate of Pius XI, many Catholic groups went under such
names as "Reign of Christ," "Christ the King" and "Regnum Christi."

were before because now our work has God's seal: struggle, opposition and persecutions.

How much the Lord loves us! We knew it would turn out this way because in unity it's Jesus in our midst and He can even die, but He always rises. He is the Holy of Holies who can never die, though we who are united in His name are so unworthy of so much grace.

In these trials our sense of values has been strengthened and we've seen that nothing outside of *holiness* matters.

You can't always have approvals; you can't always have the souls that once followed us. But you can always be holy, even when you're covered from head to toe in struggles and you seem to be dead. You seem to be dead, for when you're dead because of the divine Will, you're alive.

So let's become holy and be always more worthy of the Ideal that God's given to us. Remember that we must be the Ideal — we the living Ideal, we the living unity with God and with neighbor.

And then ... forward along the Fiery path that the Lord has indicated for us.

Remember it. "If you are what you should be you will put all of Italy on fire." [57]

This morning we were talking with a Father Provincial of the Conventuals in Umbria. He purposely stopped by in Trent to hear about this movement that was spreading in Italy. He was enthusiastic and has a whole forest of souls that follow him. Just think: aside from the convents in Umbria and aside from Assisi, the friars of all the other convents run parishes, poor parishes that are deprived of spiritual assistance due to the disastrous scarcity of priests.

Now he'd like us to bring this Ideal to all these cities and spread it everywhere. And so he's asked us to go. We promised and we'll all go. Indeed, those of us who won't be able to make the journey will have to go in spirit, because we're all one and wherever one of us is, all of us must be, feeling the challenges with her, the challenges of the apostolate as well as the need for prayers. It's like what happens in the human body. As the hand works, the stomach must digest what's been eaten. And without this effort, the hand's action would quickly decrease. And so, all of us who belong to the "Mary" Unity should form a oneness. We must form Mary, our Heavenly Mother. Then let it be Her to go forth

57. See Letter 10.

bringing the Word of God to all places. Let it be her to gather around her all the souls, brothers and sisters, children of the same Mother. Let Her work through us, us united in the Name of Jesus.

Then, let us leave everything to Her. She'll do everything well.

More good news: We read in a great magazine called *"Focolare"* that a certain Father Beda has the same Ideal as we. And he wants to spread it everywhere. According to him, the unity of all Catholics would be the only way to solve the serious problems of the present times. Thanks be to God!

Chiara

A Gospel Cure

Letter of August 17, 1948
to an unidentified consecrated religious

Speaking to a religious whom she hardly knows, Chiara explains to her the practice of the Word of Life and signs with three asterisks.

The bishop of Assisi whom she mentions was Bishop Giuseppe Placido M. Nicolini, OSB (see Letter 48).

August 17, 1948

I was so pleased to receive your letter in which you expressed your remembrance and ... unity.

Yes, may the Heavenly Mother whose daughters we are, consume us in the tightest unity, as She forms within us Her most beloved Son: *Jesus Forsaken.*

We've met in life, coming from such different paths, both of us projected toward the same Love. And that Love should make us One.

I didn't speak to you, dearest sister, about the practical side of our unity and I would like to say something about it today in writing.

We've come to realize that this world is in need of a cure...

a cure of the Gospel, because only the Good News is capable of providing the life that the world doesn't have.

This is why we live the *Word of Life*.

Every two months the Bishop of Assisi sends us a word taken from the Holy Scriptures and we live it in the present moment of our life.

We "incarnate" it in us to the point of becoming that word. One Word of the Gospel is equal to all others because it contains all of the Truth, just as a tiny piece of the Sacred Host contains all of Jesus.

One word is enough to sanctify ourselves, to be another Jesus. We live many words of Holy Scripture through time, and they remain forever a legacy that our soul must accept.

The Word of Life for August is: "Not everyone who says to me, 'Lord, Lord,' will enter the kingdom of heaven, but only the one who does the will of my Father who is in heaven" (Mt 7:21).

This is the light that illuminates all the souls who belong to unity until the end of August. Then we'll have another.

Our job, our life, is to live it in the present moment of our life. And everyone can live it, whatever our calling, age, gender, or background, because Jesus is Light for every person that comes into the world.

With this simple method we re-evangelize our souls and the world through them. Whoever does the truth comes to this Light!

Try to live it and you'll find complete perfection there. And just as you are content each morning to receive that particular Host without desiring another, be filled up and satisfied by this month's particular Word and you'll discover as Saint Francis did: "the hidden manna of miraculous fragrance!"

In this way, and only in this way, doing the truth, we are able to love. Otherwise love is just empty sentimentalism. Whereas real Love is *Christ Jesus,* it's the Truth, it's the Gospel!

May we be living Gospels, Words of Life, many other Jesuses! Only in this way will we really love Him, and we'll imitate Mary Most Holy, the Mother of Light, of the Word: the living Word.

We have no other book but the Gospel, no other science or art.
It is only there that you discover Life.
And those who find it never die.
My dearest Sister, I don't know if I've explained myself well.

I abandon these words that I've written to the Holy Spirit. When the Lord wants, if He wants, we'll meet again. Meanwhile let's dream only of being united with Him. United with Him directly, *reliving Him;* with Him in our neighbor, *making ourselves one with their pain, tears, torments, concerns, joys, fatigue, efforts and toiling.*

In this unity we'll have total peace and *perfect joy,* which was promised to those who live unity, by the sweet Jesus before He died.

May we gather this treasure into our hearts. As a Father, a Spouse, and a true Friend, He'll procure our perfect enjoyment, by the blood that He shed for us. Is there any greater Love? I leave you in the infinite Love of God as I invoke upon you from our Heavenly Mother all the Fire of the Spouse.

* * *

Letter 51

We Should Be Afraid
of Everyone But Him

Letter of September 2, 1948
to Father Bonaventura, OFM CAP.

This letter is marked by unity in God and pure love for Jesus Forsaken, who is the Way (see Jn 14:6).
Chiara signs "Silvia L."

Father Bonaventura,

I saw you yesterday. You might be at Malè today. I'm in Ortisei. But the distance doesn't prevent me from bringing your soul into mine.

Yes, because your intimate sufferings, your concerns, your fears have become my own. Jesus knows. I constantly entrust you to His Heart so that you don't make Him suffer more. Jesus suffers as He watches you suffer, after having given you — with such infinite pain! there upon the cross — the possibility of being full of joy. He'd be more joyful, Father, if you hid the eyes of your soul within His, deep within him, where he suffered the most acute abandonment known to Heaven or earth, and if you whispered to him those words that are so consoling to His Heart: "Jesus, I rejoice that I am similar to You; I rejoice that You relive Your cry within me; I want my life to be your living cry, so that I may draw countless souls to you. *This is what I want."*

And do this without analyzing the pain, without understanding if … this … or that … every suffering was in Him! Our joy is already complete, knowing that we carry within us, in our soul or in our body, that pure gold, which is suffering. It alone enables us to love Jesus with pure love. And we *always* find Jesus beneath suffering.

Pardon me, Father, if I dare to write these things to you. But Jesus allows a sister to write to her brother in Jesus, informing him that Jesus suffers at seeing him suffer. Come on, come on, Father: Get moving! *Break* whatever is keeping you tied to yourself. Do it with courage. A plunge … into the Heart of Jesus. What are you afraid of?

It's not like you're starting just any way. You're plunging into *the* Way which is Jesus. We should be afraid of everyone but Him. Continue today what the Will of God interrupted yesterday. Today — a first Friday — I'll cast you again into that Divine Heart, the center of the Unity of all hearts.

May He grant your soul rest, impetus and a burning zeal. I place you in that Heart and, in that Heart, it's possible for there to be unity (especially through deep prayer) between your soul and mine. Yes, Father, because I didn't hesitate to say it to you last time — I would really like you to pray for me. My mission requires me to ask for help and support, especially Heavenly support. Will you?

Bless me.

Silvia L.

Stay with us, please, praying for our visit to Rome – *Viva Jesus!*

Letter 52

See The Mud Transformed Into Gold

Letter of September 5, 1948
to Carmelina Anagni

By this time, Chiara's heart and mind are pervaded with the logic of the Gospel: death is life, wretchedness is a combustible that can be given to Jesus so that He might transform it into a fire of mercy.

Chiara refers to the difficulties that she mentioned in Letter 47 and in that of July of the same year, Letter 48, to the members of the nascent movement, where she announces "it was a full victory."

"That all be one!"
September 5, 1948

Dearest Carmelina,

I'm writing in answer to your last letter and to all the other letters that I was so grateful to receive.

You tell me about the bitterness that assails you because of your infidelities and because of the situation in your family.

Carmelina, will you do what I say?

Then you will see the mud transformed into gold, difficulty into peace.

Listen: Jesus feels a great need that His mercy be put to use. Well then, *make Him happy* and each time you feel the weight of your wretchedness, *give it to Him*. There's nothing he wants more than to *consume our wretchedness* in the fire of His mercy. He's made for this, because He's a Savior.

And you who can procure so many miseries for him to burn, why are you sad? Instead of looking at your own soul, why don't you look at His thirst for consuming, annihilating misery?

How few are the souls that understand this. And so they keep on their soul a putrid pile of refuse, which, if it were given to Jesus, could be transformed into Mercy! Fire!

It's like putting straw on the fire, it becomes fire. Therefore, from now on, whenever you feel oppressed by your misery, you'll rejoice at having something to give to Jesus that he can add to his fire.

Understand?

Then, regarding your family situation, *don't worry*. Jesus said: "Cast *every* worry on me": *every*: so yours too. And Jesus will take care of it. If you worry, it means that you don't trust Him. When we know that something has been put in good hands, we no longer worry about it. Continuing to worry would be an offense against the person to whom we had entrusted the thing. So tomorrow at the Holy Mass turn to Jesus with trust (He can do everything!) and say to Him: "Jesus, take care of my affair." But throw away all worry in order to continue to demonstrate to Him your trust.

I certainly put your cousin, the new priest, in unity. Oh! The Lord loves priests so much! And they're so important! And I'll always pray for him. Your little sister will also be helped by my prayer. Be certain of this. The 12th of this month I'll be in Rome, but only for three days. My Spiritual Father has already told me that due to my unstable health, I will only be able to deal in general matters with the Fathers. I'll obey him. But perhaps Jesus will make things work out differently. We'll see.

Now that our victory has been complete, we've begun to go at gallop speed. Therefore, I'm certain that I'll pass by once again wherever there are souls of the Unity — and soon.

We're always only following what the Divine Will desires and Jesus fulfills all our desires. May Jesus soon consume us all in one.

Always pray for your Bishop.[58]

I always remember him with great veneration.

Jesus loves us. May we love Him with deeds, sacrifices, humiliations, trust, and unity!

Chiara

Never Desire Perfection, Desire to Love Him

Letter of September 8, 1948
to Father Bonaventura, OFM CAP.

This consecrated religious had confided to Chiara what he was going through in his soul. She responds with precise counsels on holiness.

It is not known who Father Gammaria is, nor for what decision it is necessary to pray.

"That all be one!"

Reverend Father Bonaventura, dearest brother in Jesus,

Today, today of all days — the Nativity of Mary — I received your letter with your promise of a Holy Mass already fulfilled. You couldn't have given me a bigger gift. The Mass!

And that glimmer of light and peace that were born in you, I take also as a gift from Mary, your Mother and mine. It was Mary's doing.

---

58. Bishop Giovanni Battista Piasentini.

How much joy Jesus gave to me through your letter! *Jesus is there.*
I found Him in your thirst for "life," in the optimism contained in it that swells throughout it here and there, and especially in the peace generated by the desire to love Him more and more.

Be completely certain that — as long as I'm with Jesus (And how could I ever leave Him? In Paradise I'll have Him even more.) — I'll never stop following your soul with a watchful eye and sisterly care. Oh! I know the value of a priest.

And I gather and gather souls and souls in my heart of the Bride of Christ because I feel this heart to be like an opening through which, passing through it, you go directly to Jesus. And Jesus, the Bridegroom, takes care of all His Bride's affairs. Not only is He able to carry, sanctify and unite all the souls, but He *wants* them, He desires them with His dying breath.

Yes, Father, that interior dissatisfaction was God's voice, or rather a "permission of God."

Jesus let you feel what it means to live without *loving.* People alone with themselves are always bored because in themselves they find only nothingness.

He is Love, Fullness, Joy, Peace, Prosperity and Riches!

And if our soul isn't one with Him, then it's nothing.

And now that you've taken the plunge, oh! Father, keep going!

Don't try to determine by yourself whether or not you're going forward. It's subtle pride. Always look at Him: Jesus says: No one who puts a hand to the plow and looks back is fit for service in the kingdom of God (see Lk 9:62).

He, your singular passion and Father Bonaventura, lost, dead, annulled in Him.

Never desire perfection. Desire to love Him. And love Him *moment by moment* by accomplishing the Divine Will with all your heart, all your strength, and all your mind. Never anything polluted in your soul. Let everything be "pure love," that is, a sincere intention to express love of God.

Feel this Supernatural Reality which is God, as the only Object of the affection of your heart, as the only Father, Brother, Friend, Consoler, Physician, Medicine, Spouse of your soul. And like a child resting on his mother, don't rest on anything but Him.

Let those words spoken by Saint Francis in prayer be true for your heart, most especially your heart, for everything in our life follows the heart: *My God, my All!*

You'll never find what your soul is longing for on earth. At times, a soul believes it's found something spiritual to lean on in a spiritual father. But blessed is the soul that God allows to understand that the spiritual father is nothing more than a voice to obey. The Person our soul desires (for we are human beings) is no one but *Jesus*.

Rip out of your soul anything that is not self-forgetfulness ... and place Jesus within this soul that doesn't know how to be alone. He's the Beauty that our soul is searching for, the Light that the mind craves, the Force: He is *Love*.

And after you've placed Him in your heart to be your *All*, tell Him that *we are all His forever.*

And — to love Him — start by listening to *His Word* and putting it into practice. *His Words* are not like the words in books that are so watered down and never pure gold, pure life, pure love like His. And *act:* "Whoever *does* the truth will come to the Light" (See Jn 3:21).

And listen to this Word of Light, which blossoms in us after we have lived it. Share it with those who are able to understand it, in order not to leave them in the "light" but to transform them into charity, into love.

And gather more light from this action and then share *that...*

This is the game of love always being played by the Most Holy Trinity:

Light-Life
Love

among the souls united in Jesus.

When we meet again, Father, I *must* find you feeling better.

Jesus awaits your love and you can't make Him wait. Do everything that the Will of God requires. You have the grace for it *and life is short.*

Jesus waits with His holiness for the sanctification of very many souls. You can't make Him wait.

And if you don't have Light, oh! Father, ask me, for Heaven's sake — for whatever you need. I see that I would be able to resolve your every darkness with the Light of Jesus. Don't ask if I'll have patience to continue cultivating that tiny seed. I won't allow myself to be at peace until I see Jesus fully formed in you. Then I'll abandon you to

Jesus alone, for then you'll be *one* with my soul and I always abandon my soul to *Jesus alone*.

You shared your life's odyssey with me. It's precisely the logical course that Jesus takes.

At first He gives us the illusion and the happiness of having found *Him*. Then, so that nothing human can block the Work of God, He permits periods of darkness, disturbing moments, of disgust, so that we can see what we are, and aware of our nothingness and of our wretchedness, we might throw ourselves again into Him, with total trust only in Him.

Therefore, Father, see your life as being guided by a Divine Hand. Just when you perhaps felt most abandoned, Jesus was carving out the foundation in order to then construct the House = Himself.

Even when building houses it seems rather contradictory to dig down when we have to build up. Similarly in the soul, it's first necessary to create an emptiness, to empty it of everything else until there is a total *emptiness*. This is why we are passionate about Jesus Forsaken! Following Him means: *emptying ourselves*. And you, Father, must second this action of God in your soul. Listen to each inspiration of Grace and you'll see that Jesus will always tell you to demolish.

For today I leave you in the Abandoned Heart of our Crucified Love.

May the Sorrowful Mother resurrect you to a holy life that is truly *all love*.

Bless me.

Sister Chiara

Remember to greet Father Giammaria especially for me. Jesus loves Father Giammaria greatly. We must love him too. I'll remember both of you especially between the decisive days of the 12th and 17th.

Living the Word That Makes Us One

Letter of October 23, 1948
to Father Raffaele Massimei, OFM CONV.

Here Chiara requests that Father Massimei meet Pallotine Father Joseph Liegle, the spiritual director of Palmira Frizzera, one of the first focolarine.

She mentions Graziella De Luca and Natalia Dalla Piccola, who were also among her first companions.

For Father Veuthey, OFM CONV. and Father Beda see Letters 35 and 49.

She describes the practice of the Word of Life as being in function of unity.

Trent, October 23, 1948

"Whoever wants to come after me
must deny himself, take up his cross,
and follow me." (Jesus)[59]

Father Massimei,

I spoke just now with a Pallotine Father who came from Germany and has been staying in Rome for some time, since he was appointed spiritual father at the International College of the Pallottine Missionaries on Pettinari Way. His name is Father Giuseppe Liegle. He was at one time the spiritual father of Palmira and he had pointed her in the direction of our Ideal, which he deeply cherished.

He's enthusiastic about unity and says that it's the Ideal that Jesus desires for the present age.

He'll certainly be going to see you. I only gave him your address,

---

59. Mt 16:24.

and since he'll be able to work with us for as much time as he can, if you could, Father, introduce him to the members of the Unity; first and foremost to Father Leone Veuthey and to Father Beda, of course.

I think he'd also be willing to help out with translations, since he's German.

Up here everything's fine.

We're going at gallop speed.

In the next few days I'll go to Padua and to Rovigo. A Christian community is forming in Treviso.

Every day there are new souls being sent to us by the Lord, and all of them want to know more and to do something.

How good He is!

May we be united, Father, in the Name of the Lord, living the Word of life that makes us one.

I'll tell you a little "parable" or example that could help the souls to learn unity better.

You know that Graziella and Natalia were operated on for appendicitis. Yesterday the doctor removed Graziella's stitches. I thought: "Look how strange ... now the wound stays closed by itself. Indeed the two sides of the wound have united and become a single piece of flesh." I immediately thought of grafting plants, where the two parts that have been peeled make contact with the living part of the branch and become one. Why? Because the two parts that make contact are both "alive."

When are two souls able to be consumed in one? When they are "alive," that is, when the human has been peeled away, when their own personality has been peeled away and, through the living Word of Life, incarnating it, they are living words. Two living words can consume themselves in one. If one of them is not alive, the other one cannot unite itself.

The more I go ahead, the more I see the beauty of the Word of Life! It's like a little pill that concentrates within it everything that Jesus brought to earth: the Gospel message. There isn't love without truth because charity is truth in action. (Here again ... it's always the Most Holy Trinity.)

Goodbye for today, Father!

Other tasks are awaiting me.

Greet all those who are living and those who are not, so that they might begin to live. When the Lord desires it, he'll provide the apartment for us. Meanwhile, we see that it wouldn't be good to have it.

Always with you in the most perfect unity.

I just remembered that your feast day is coming soon. Raphael = Medicine of God!

Oh! May you be so! May you be the physician of Unity: healing, cutting, operating ... healing all the souls of Unity from down there with prayer and action, everywhere: being Jesus = Living Word.

Saint Raphael's day will be all for you: Holy Communion, Holy Mass and living...

It's the wish that's ever ancient, ever new.

Give me your blessing.

Sister Chiara

 **55**

Don't Tell Me ...
You Don't Have Time

Letter of November 4, 1948
to a group from Anagni

This letter shows how Chiara asks everything from those who begin to follow Christ, just as she asks everything of herself. She repudiates those who are lukewarm, in accordance with the sentence from Revelations: "So, because you are lukewarm, and neither cold nor hot, I am about to spit you out of my mouth." (3:16). This letter appears as a small guidebook for the apostolate, as she indicates the characteristics of a person who would be a soul of fire.

Dearest Sisters of Anagni,

The memory of you is always alive in our hearts, and up here in Trent we live in expectation of the day when we can live close — close to each other and be able to share our ideas and all the gifts that God gives to us.

Since I'm writing to all of you, let me tell you something that's in my heart, which will certainly be useful to you.

It's God's will that all of Anagni fall into the furnace of Love of Jesus' Heart.

Therefore, let's take advantage of every possibility. May we accomplish to perfection the Will of God that God asks of each one of us. Then, seeing our efforts and the partial results of our loving activity (we're always limited!), Jesus, who is Infinite, will open new horizons, totally new possibilities and cast us into every field of human society, like fiery embers that will fill every place with Fire.

But this is Jesus' work. The important thing for us is that we do our part; that is, to accomplish the will of God upon us.

It's God's command that we love Him with all our heart; that is, that we do the will of God with all our heart, which right now is to *love each other* and to love the neighbor who is at our side moment by moment, to such a point and with such momentum that our neighbors will be swept away by our Ideal and constrained by love *to love God with their whole heart.*

My sisters, Jesus is pleased knowing that another three sisters are united to you, as Carmelina has written to me, but at the same time He weeps because you've won over so few to His Heart.

Forgive me for talking to you in this way. I should first reproach myself, but allow me to say what I think!

Don't tell me that the people from Anagni are hard, that you don't have the skills, that you don't have time, and so forth. It's not true: *Love conquers all!*[60]

It's love that's lacking in our hearts! And too often we believe that loving God means offering hours of adoration, going to religious places, praying for long hours, etc. Religion isn't only this, my sisters!

It's going out in search of the lost sheep after having cared for the others! *It's making yourself all things to all people! Loving every soul that draws*

---

60. Virgil, *Bucolics,* 10, 69.

near to us as we love our own, loving them in practical and concrete ways; loving them strongly and with sweetness. It's loving their soul as we love our own and desiring for their soul what we desire for ours. It's being surrounded by a myriad of hearts that are awaiting from ours the word that gives life; it's loving, loving by denying ourselves, *our own ways of seeing things, our own habits.*

The Lord is in urgent need of souls like these: *souls of Fire!*, free of "spiritual problems" — eternal obstacles to love! — who've burnt everything, and long to burn everyone else in the fire. He needs souls who are able to love each other with an open mind, who go beyond their own small circle and interests, and interest themselves only in the interests of others — before *their* own.

He needs souls who love each other so much that they submit everything to *Jesus among them* because they maintain Him always more alive with their ever growing communion of spiritual and material goods.

Even the slightest thing that you keep for yourself can be a threat to unity.

Share everything, everything that is the will of God.

Jesus awaits these souls, so that they can be light for everyone in the house. Bright, burning – chandeliers!

Yet how few of them He finds.

A vocation itself is egoism for most people. They wait with longing to follow their own path, to release themselves from the burden of the family and other concerns.

And they don't realize that they should rather remain there *to love God* by loving their own. Poor Jesus!

And this is why the world is so cold. The fault is ours!

My sisters, let's get to it!

Let's sincerely love. Let's enlarge the circle of unity to the largest possible quantity of souls.

This is love of God.

Chiara

Wishes of Infinite Love to everyone.

Carmelina,

Rest assured that I'll pray for your intention.

The Word of Life is: "If anyone wants to come after me, let him deny himself, take up his cross and follow me."

I've sent these few thoughts so that you can share them with everyone. Let's be very united.
May the Word of God make us holy.

Chiara

Letter 56

You Give Us Paradise on Earth

Letter of December 27, 1948
to Father Bonaventura, OFM CAP.

The discovery of "Jesus in the midst" (see Letter 36) is the arrival point of Chiara's spiritual journey and its fulfillment. This letter, which is supplemented with practical advice, could be described as a hymn to Jesus in our midst and a testimony that Chiara's calling, her burning desire, is to provide a way for this presence to manifest itself: "For where two or three are gathered in my name, there am I in the midst of them" (Mt 18:20).

For Father Girolomo, see Letter 44.

The "four hearts" included Father Bonaventura as well as Father Topi, who later would become Bishop of Pompeii.

Trent, December 27, 1948
That all be one!

Father Bonaventura,

Truly the Lord is great, great, great!

Your little letter today filled us with joy. And so now also in the International College at 159 *Sicilia Way* there's Jesus in the midst of four hearts already made *one heart!*

"Good Jesus, Infinite Love, who lives among the four hearts of our

134

brothers in Rome, receive our happiness! Once again we can only be silent as we watch what you are doing. We can't but remain in silent adoration of your burning Love!

We who for years have carried You *among* us and who have witnessed the miracles of your Power, cannot but cry out to you:

Grow giant *among* those priestly *hearts* and *from*[61] those hearts extend the loving caress of your Love to all the souls that surround your small Reign. Gather into it as many as you can! We want to share with every soul that draws near to ours all the happiness we have in Unity, which you have given to us by dying! We can't keep it only for ourselves, because many, many are hungry and thirsty for this total peace, this infinite joy!

Make use of us. Pulverize our heart, our body, our entire being, so that You alone may live in <u>us</u>. We're not afraid of anything. We're ready for everything, any suffering, the throes of death.

We've *chosen* You in Your maximum abandonment upon the Cross as our Everything in life … and You give us Paradise on earth.

You're God, God, God."

Father, I don't have time today to write you as much as I would like. I'd never finish… But I find peace and serenity knowing that *Jesus is among you* and that He'll tell you everything He said to us during these years that we've been living a life of unity.

Oh! If you only knew, if you only knew! At times our heart is so full that it nearly bursts! What happiness I feel knowing that Jesus — our only Treasure, only Wisdom, only Joy, only Source of Life (of that Life that we like!) — is among you just *as* He's among us! Now you're not lacking anything!

Let's just be careful of Satan's attacks on Unity. I speak from experience: he'll try *every trick in the book* to destroy Unity. He knows that Unity is omnipotent and that the souls consumed in One are absolutely lost to him.

And so: *"above all"*[62] (even if this "all" includes the most beautiful things, the most sacred things: like praying, celebrating the Holy Mass, etc, etc.) be one! Then it will no longer be you who acts, prays, or celebrates … but always *Jesus in you!*

---

61. Underlined three times.
62. "Above all, maintain constant love for one another…" (1 Pt 4:8).

135

Unity is the training ground for those who would be holy. It's the triumph of charity, of Love. It's Paradise already achieved, even though we are still on this earth and therefore always "on the field" so that we remain *one* and consume other souls in *one!*

Your first responsibility is that all the Capuchins be *one!* while never excluding the other neighbors that the Lord places near to you.

Die, die *completely* in Jesus among you!

Have everything in common: give all that you have to each other *with generosity!*

Then, one by one, Jesus will consume the brothers who live around you, and He'll prepare those who are far away for Unity.

Just as an object that draws near to a whirlpool in the sea is inexorably drawn into its vortex, (the whirlpool is formed by two currents! And isn't this also a symbol of unity?). Likewise, any soul that meets *Jesus* (Jesus among us) will be inexorably lost in his Love. I hope that the *Jesus among you* casts the net into the great sea of Capuchins and that every day there will be a miraculous catch!

May 1949 be rich in every blessing for everyone in the Unity.

The brothers and sisters of Trent are overjoyed to greet Unity's new little Reign.

Sister Chiara

See you soon! (We're in contact by letter with Father Girolamo and friends.)

What Have We Done
to Receive Such a Gift?

Letter of February 17, 1949
to four consecrated religious men
Chiara doesn't invite, but commands these men to rejoice over their pruning, otherwise they haven't understood unity. She again underscores the unbreakable link between Jesus Forsaken and unity.
She signs S. C. (Sister Chiara)

February 17, 1949
"That all be One!"

Brothers in Unity, in Jesus, our All,

How it makes us rejoice so deeply in our hearts to see how much the Lord loves you!

For a few months now the new sun of Charity has risen on the horizon of your life and melted you into one heart so that the Lord — already certain of your faithfulness — now puts your virtue to the test.

Yesterday, when I learned that the Divine Will, the fatherly Hand of God had begun the salutary and necessary work of pruning the growing plant, I could hardly believe it. I was expecting it, but not so soon! And Jesus immediately made me see with how much predilection He loves you. He loves you. My little Brothers, if anything has taken up residence in your hearts that doesn't resemble joy for what is happening, then that heart must admit that it hasn't understood *Unity*.

What is happening to you is the logical consequence of the Ideal that we've proposed for ourselves.

It is *Jesus* who is among you who are united in His name. You form *Jesus*, and Jesus cannot but live life as Jesus does!

He said that the small vine tree that bore fruit would be pruned so that it might bear even better fruits. And so, aren't you rejoicing with the fullness of joy at seeing such care on the part of the Father for you?

Have you still not understood that the greatest Ideal the human heart could desire — Unity — is only a dream, a chimera, if the one who wants it doesn't have as his only treasure in life *Jesus who is abandoned by all, even by His Father?*

This apparent detachment, this forced disunity from your brothers and sisters outside the college who live and suffer for your same Ideal, isn't this perhaps a little bit of Jesus Forsaken for you? Perhaps this is the first time He's appeared to your souls made into a single soul and asked you to love Him with all your heart through perfect adherence to the Divine Will by having — as your only desire — whatever He wants, even if it's bitter, even if it's painful, even if it has the taste of exile.

It's only by *wholeheartedly* embracing Jesus Forsaken, all wounded in body and soul and covered by darkness, that our soul will be formed by *Unity.*

Oh! If only I could pour into your heart, brother, the entire mystery of his Abandonment, at least inasmuch as Jesus in his mercy has revealed it to me!

Herein lies the secret of the greatest and ultimate dream of our Jesus, "that all be one!"

We and you, as sharers in this infinite Sorrow, will contribute effectively to the Unity of all the brothers! Jesus is so happy because of what we're doing! The Blessed Mother is so happy there above seeing Her Jesus in <u>us</u>! How happy our brother Saints in glory, seeing us already so inundated here below by the fullness of Jesus' Light and Joy! What have we done to receive such a gift?… I don't know how to say it to you as I'd like, as my heart, the heart of your sisters would like, but our Happiness is complete knowing that *Jesus is among you*, that He already has His little flock there inside, the little flock that has been given the *Kingdom!*

Keep *Jesus among you*, I implore you, by always being *united in His Name* so that you never do anything but His will and, by doing so, you'll respond to Love with love.

Remain in his love — loving each other as He has loved each one of you — and then His and your Ideal will triumph and your entire college will be a Hearth — a living temple of the Holy Spirit — and you'll be the *living* stones.

February 18, 1949

Tempestuous winds are blowing all around us, too. But we never lament that Jesus seems to be asleep on the little boat of *Unity*.

No, no! He's always watching and at the opportune moment will beautifully appear, bright and compassionate toward all the hearts that are enveloped in uncertainty, doubt and division.

Together with you, we believe in Love.

For the entire Unity,

S.C.

If You Divide, You'll Perish

Letter of May 4, 1949
to a group in Sardinia

Accompanied by Lia Brunet and Valeria Ronchetti, Chiara went to Sardinia in April 1949. She had been invited to Sassari by the Diana family (Gesuina and her mother) and she stayed at Sanluri in the province of Cagliari. She went to meet Giovanna Giua, a young widow, known to Father Casimiro da Peralo, OFM CAP., who had moved to Sardinia. On her way back to Rome Chiara wrote this letter to the entire community.

Igino Giordani, whom she mentions, was the journalist and deputy in the Constituent Assembly, who later became a married focolarino and played an important role in the Movement.

Chiara offers valuable advice on how to create an authentic

Christian community.
Although unsigned, the letter is certainly Chiara's.

(NB. Please spread this letter around to all the brothers and sisters, both consecrated and lay.)

Rome, May 4, 1949
"Blessed are those who mourn,
for they will be comforted·" (Mt. 5:4)

Dearest Brothers and Sisters in Jesus,

Here we are in the capital again, the heart of Catholicism.

In just a few hours the plane carried us far, very far away from you, but Love which united us keeps us among all of you brothers and sisters in Sassari, Sanluri, Cagliari, etc. And we carry you here to the mainland where there are already hundreds and thousands of brothers who know you and love you and wait for you.

What a divine Ideal, Unity! Who will ever separate us from the love of Christ? And, if we are all united by this love, who will ever separate us from each other? Not the sea, not the distance, not the dangers ... nothing! We love Sardinia as much as you do because, having known your hearts, so burning, generous and brave, we are certain that your land is blessed by God.

The Ideal that we proclaimed to you and are now proclaiming all over the peninsula will unite all your hearts that have been made for the heights. And you, you Sardinians, will give the world an example of brotherhood, of mutual solidarity, of a Christian community as no one has ever done before.

As soon as we returned to Rome we found everyone waiting for us.

Oh! I wish all of you could spend a day in the glowing atmosphere of the Community! And after I've spoken about you to those closest to us, so that they can love, appreciate, and feel close to you, I'm going to speak to a Jesuit priest who has a talk show on Vatican Radio.

This morning I went to the Jesuit Generalate and I spoke with him for about an hour...

Conclusion: He couldn't stop saying how wonderful the Ideal is and that Jesus would want to spread it to Ireland, England, America and even ... India!

And we'll go everywhere, won't we, our brothers? But since we don't have bi-location and life is short and it's urgent that the Kingdom of God advances, Jesus will raise up, especially among you, such Flame and Light that you yourselves will be the instruments of His Glory in your own environments and beyond.

God wants it!

Prepare, working with each other in perfect brotherly love. Go out for the conquest of all the souls around you and, when they come to visit you, make their hearts beat with yours for the same Ideal.

Try to get to know each of them personally, so that you can understand which ones truly feel like brothers. Help each other in forming Jesus in your hearts and soon Sassari, Sanluri, and Cagliari will have an actual Community.

I met people of all vocations among you, of every age, both men and women.

Oh! I implore the mothers to feel and act like mothers for all the boys and girls that the Lord touched with His Light. I beg the fathers to be fathers for everyone, and the young people to be brothers and sisters.

And let there be perfect brotherhood, understanding and helping among all of you secular and religious, sisters, brothers and elderly.

See Jesus in each other and don't allow any pretexts that could destroy your unity that the Lord has brought to you.

If you're all united, your cities will be *one* with the triumph of Love, the absence of sin, and the Glory of Jesus. If you divide, you'll perish.

And always keep in mind: We love all of you with the very Heart of Jesus; we love each and every one of you as dearest brothers and dearest sisters. What is ours is yours.

You in Sassari greet Jesus for us, who is living in the little chapel of the Sisters in Gesuina's house, where I brought Him the concerns of your city every morning. Let this house be the center of the Community and let it welcome every brother and sister as Jesus who enters.

All of you in Sanluri stay united to the brothers in Sassari. They'll visit you. Build eternal relationships, for our Ideal begins here below and continues forever. Religious and laity, rich and poor, always be one in heart.

Greetings from everyone in Rome to all of you whom Valeria visited in Cagliari. We've come to know your heart and the Lord God will perform wonders through you if you're united.

Be always more worthy of Jesus: He lives among you *so that all may be one!*

Everyone greets you and feels one with you! Be united on Friday at five o'clock as our brother, Igino Giordani speaks at the Gregorian University to an audience of a thousand people. I'll send you his talk so that you can discuss it and share it among our brothers and sisters.

Let's keep praying for each other.

To all of you I send all the Heart of Jesus among us!

*L*etter 59

Jesus Among Souls Does Miracles

Letter of June 26, 1949
to Father Giovanni Pinesi

Father Pinesi, the parish priest at Saint Philomena's Church in Pescara, had recently come to know the Movement. This letter is a little treatise on community life.

Rome, June 26, 1949

Reverend Father John, dearest brother in Jesus,

It was a great joy for us to receive your letter which was also signed by the other souls in unity. Yes, the fire continues in all directions and no one will be able to stop it. The Fire that Jesus brought to the earth, devouring Fire that consumes everything that isn't God: *Jesus in our midst*. And, *through us*, He lights it in the world once again.

What a mission Jesus has given to us: As the Father has sent Him, so Jesus sends us, having sanctified us in the truth.

The Word of Life is our hidden treasure, what cleanses and consumes us in one with *Jesus and with each other*. And no one could break such a bond.

Tell the souls in Pescara that we're more united than they could ever imagine. Tell them that they should be consumed in One, sharing with each other all the treasures they possess, especially the spiritual ones, so that it may be Jesus in their midst to make them holy. And tell them that they should have their gaze set on the whole city, for everything will be won over by Jesus among them if they're united.

Jesus among souls does miracles. Conversions are the order of the day and the revolutions taking place in people's hearts are more and more frequent: It's the fiery wave of Love that overturns everything. It's the Light of Jesus.

The important thing is that we remain united and that we share everything as much as possible through the wireless telephone of the Communion of Saints, and by every external means that the Lord God places at our disposal, that our letters may bring ahead the advancement of the Fire and Jesus be given all the Glory in the world. But *if it's Jesus among us to give the glory, then it will certainly be great glory.*

Greet all the brothers and sisters for us; they're as dear to us *as* we are to ourselves. Give us your blessing as a minister of Love and friend of Jesus.

Sister Chiara

The whole community of Rome sends greetings to all of you.

143

L*etter* 60

Let Us Believe and It Shall Be So

Letter of June 17, 1949
to the community of Rome

This letter is co-signed by three of Chiara's first companions.
The small apartment of which she speaks, located in the
Garbatella quarter, was the first focolare in Rome.
The Holy Year was held in 1950.
Chiara talks about the "sweet mystery of unity" and indicates
the Word of Life as the means for achieving it.

June 17, 1949

Dearest Brothers and Sisters of Unity,

Livio and your three sisters are on their way to Trent for a month or so.

Before going, they wanted to send their greetings to each and every one of you, and to leave you with something to remember them by.

We've learned that the souls of Unity are being called "incendiaries," a title that is somewhat unmerited by us who, though we have been given so much light by God, have so often extinguished this sacred Fire of God's Love within our own souls and in the souls of others, with the coldness of our egoism and the meanness of our thinking.

Still, the name is nice and could be a goal for us to strive for.

And it could become a reality if we're faithful to the Ideal that the Lord God has given to us.

If we are united — and never break this unity for any reason within us or outside of us — *Jesus will always be in our midst* and He will set everything on Fire. He came only to bring Fire on the earth and doesn't desire anything but that it should become a blaze (see Lk 12:49). And whoever is near to Him is near to the Fire!

Of course, Rome isn't like other cities where the Community is more visible and can be more deeply formed because of the ease in communicating (it's by knowing each other and loving each other that souls are set on Fire); but for souls that *believe in love* there are no difficulties. All of us to whom the Lord God has given to understand the sweet mystery of Unity will be united to every other soul of the Unity, even the ones we don't know. We'll be in communication with them and they with us, through the Heart of Jesus in which all are part.

And when the Will of God has us encounter a brother or a sister in this city of Rome, which can seem like a desert even though it's so crowded with people, let us allow our spirit to expand and to receive the heart of that brother or sister so that *Jesus is among us* and, through our Communion, the other souls of Unity will stay faithful to the Ideal. Even from afar — those in the mountains and those by the sea — a Light will join us all together, imperceptible to the senses and ignored by the world, but more dear to God and to the souls of Unity than anything else on earth:

the Word of Life.

We can *be one* only if each of us is another Jesus,
another living Word of God.

Wherever the Lord God sends us, let us love our neighbor as ourselves because in this way we love Jesus. It's become so clear to us by now that Love is the sole purpose of our life. And with Love we'll win over other souls. And with our Ideal we'll give them all that their heart could desire, because we'll give them *Jesus.*

Thus even our resting will be fruitful to the Cause for which we were born, for which we live, and for which we will die — and no one will stop the Fire. It's the only thing in the world that matters.

The four of us here in Trent who already know most of you, have you in our heart and you are dear to us *as* we are to ourselves. And we are determined to return to you so that Jesus may see His Testament fulfilled in you and through you.

What's more: Next year will be the Holy Year. Oh, how I'd wish that all the souls would understand what I'm saying to you: Rome will be the center of the world and the souls of the entire world will go to it as to the Center of Christendom. Oh! If only alongside the beautiful churches, the glorious monuments, the palaces and hotels, the pilgrims were to find scattered here and there like flames, some true

Christians, distinguishable from everyone else only because of their love for each other and for others, with open hearts like the Heart of Jesus, disposed to help everyone, leaving everyone not only with the memory of past Christianity, but of a living Catholic religion, more alive and more beautiful and more interesting than the most beautiful mausoleums that comprise the richness of Rome.

Only "Unity" among brothers gives testimony to Christ as the Son of God.

What I'm saying to you all could seem like a dream or an illusion.

And it is, for those who trust in human beings alone. We trust in *Jesus among us* who are united, and it shall be.

Already many souls — lay people of every vocation, in international colleges and in the convents of the sisters — feel our Ideal quivering within them as the only hope: Jesus alone is the Life. If each of us lives this Fire, we'll set many others on Fire and Rome will be scattered everywhere with Flames.

When God works (and He works if we let Him), He works miracles.

Let us believe it and it shall be. And may our unshakeable faith be always crowned by works of Love.

Providence has given us a small apartment to use when we return to you, where we girls will live united so that *Jesus is among us:* the Hearth-fire. It will be the home of all the souls of Unity because what is ours is yours. There you will come to warm yourselves when the cold of the world has chilled you and the shadows of hatred and indifference have forced you to doubt and no longer believe that Love conquers all.

Be confident: Jesus among us will win over the world, and do greater things than He once did. He said so Himself.

And so, in the meantime, be watchful in *Love.*

And don't be so surprised if the world hates you. We've passed from death to life because we've loved our neighbors.

And when evening falls all around you, when your closest are about to abandon you, be glad! It's the moment of intimate union with the Only One who sustains us in Unity: Jesus Forsaken. Widen the scope of your heart then, and your mind beyond your own circle: to Trent, Naples, Sardinia, Milan, Venice, Rovigo and many other places where many brothers and sisters believe and live and love.

Write to us up here in Trent. Our address is: 2 Capuchin Square – Trent. We'll write back.

Jesus among us, our only Guide, only Master, only Father will not be lacking for anyone. Because of Him we believe in you and you can rely on us.

In the Mother of Unity,

Chiara — Giosi — Grazella — Livio.